The Joys of Parenting

Lily Foyster

BALBOA
PRESS
A DIVISION OF HAY HOUSE

Balboa Press books may be ordered through booksellers or by contacting:

Balboa Press
A Division of Hay House
1663 Liberty Drive
Bloomington, IN 47403
www.balboapress.com.au
1 (877) 407-4847

Because of the dynamic nature of the Internet, any web addresses or links contained in this book may have changed since publication and may no longer be valid. The views expressed in this work are solely those of the author and do not necessarily reflect the views of the publisher, and the publisher hereby disclaims any responsibility for them.

The author of this book does not dispense medical advice or prescribe the use of any technique as a form of treatment for physical, emotional, or medical problems without the advice of a physician, either directly or indirectly. The intent of the author is only to offer information of a general nature to help you in your quest for emotional and spiritual well-being. In the event you use any of the information in this book for yourself, which is your constitutional right, the author and the publisher assume no responsibility for your actions.

Any people depicted in stock imagery provided by Getty Images are models, and such images are being used for illustrative purposes only.
Certain stock imagery © Getty Images.

Print information available on the last page.

ISBN: 978-1-5043-1357-5 (sc)
ISBN: 978-1-5043-1358-2 (e)

Balboa Press rev. date: 07/25/2018

DEDICATION

I dedicate this book to all the young parents in my family. I know that you all believe in doing your best as a parent and in giving your children the best childhood that you possibly can; God bless you all for that. May you navigate skilfully the many challenges that parenting brings at each stage of childhood.

This book is also dedicated to all the future parents in my family too and I know that you too will be as good and devoted to your children when your time comes. I hope to be there to cheer you all on.

In addition, I dedicate this book to: Jamie and Maya, James and Matthew, Jack, Luke and Tommy, Lucy and Benjamin, Marcus and Isaac, Harry and Alex, Finn, Sebastien and Leo and to all their new cousins to come.

You are our future! See the beauty in life and may your glass always be half full. Enjoy your childhood, be proud of who you are and of your family and go forth confidently.

May life be kind to you.

I pray that you will continue to treasure each other and our family values and make this planet a better place to live in by doing whatever you can to help your fellow man and make a difference in the world.

With all my love always
Xxx

About the Author

After spending many years working with families and children, Lily Foyster shares some of her knowledge and experience in From Me To You, The Joys Of Parenting. Foyster is a successful Life coach, who lives in Perth, Western Australia, who has a passion for helping people live the best life that they can. She has a BSc (Hons) degree in health studies and is a Neuro-Linguistic Programmer and Emotional Freedom Technique Practitioner. She has twice been nominated Australian of the Year for her work. Her first book: From Me To You, The Tapestry Of Life And Its secrets was published in 2013.

Contents

Introduction

The way that we bring up this generation will be the legacy that we leave to our great grandchildren.

Let me introduce myself to you. My name is Lily. My background is in Advanced Nursing. I have worked with families and children since 1981. I have thoroughly enjoyed my work as a Nurse, Health Visitor, Specialist Practice Teacher, Nurse Practitioner (UK) and as a Child Health Nurse, in Western Australia.

It has been my privilege to work as a Post Natal Depression (PND) Specialist (UK). I am passionate about helping women who experience difficulties prior to or after giving birth. Although I was working as part of my role as a PND Specialist to help these women, I gained as much from them. They have greatly enriched my life and knowledge about this very debilitating illness. Consequently, I have spent very many years studying psychology, self-development amongst other things to help them on their way to recovery. Nowadays, I am still able to help them, but in a Life Coaching capacity.

It has always been my deep yearning to help people and my career path eventually lead me to Life Coaching which is now my great passion. I formalised my training and qualified as a Life Coach at The Life Coaching Institute, Perth, Western Australia.

I am a Neuro-Linguistic Programmer (NLP) and an Emotional Freedom Technique (EFT) Practitioner, which are very valuable to a Life Coach. I now work as a self-employed Life Coach in Perth, Western Australia.

There is nothing more satisfying than helping someone who is experiencing great difficulties than to be able to empower them and send them on the path to health, success and happiness.

I have a BSc (Hons) degree in Health Studies, which gives me an understanding about my clients' health issues, which means that I can take a holistic approach to their problems.

I was twice nominated for Australian of the Year in 2013 and 2014 for my work.

My first book was published in December 2013. It's called: *From Me To You The Tapestry Of Life And It's Secrets.*

The "From Me To You" part of the title, is there because I wanted to leave a gift here on earth for future generations, sharing the knowledge that I have accumulated over the years with others; hence that's the reason that this book is also: *From Me To You The Joys Of Parenting.*

I enjoyed writing both books, as a lot of the contents are many of the lessons that I teach my clients as a Life Coach.

The first book, *From Me To You The Tapestry Of Life And Its Secrets*, contains many exercises which can relax you and help you re-wire your brain for the better. It explains how our attitude of approach to life is key to our success; it describes how our brain works, discusses how our beliefs and values, our self-image, and the unwritten rules that we all have, how they control our life without many of us being aware about it and offers solutions. The book raises awareness about Relationships, Friends, Forgiveness, Confidence, Fear and Faith and much, much more. It is a book that many young parents can also benefit from.

Ever since I wrote that book, I have had an urge to write another to help parents, since I have had a lot of experience working with parents, children and families.

Parenting is probably one of the hardest jobs that you will ever do but also one of the most rewarding.

This book is called the "**Joys**" of parenting, not the "joy" because as any parent knows parenting brings immeasurable joy and happiness but there is also another side to parenting which can bring a lot of trials and tribulations at times. Until you become a parent, it is not possible to know the incredible joy that being a mother, or a father brings and the indescribable love that you feel for your children. It is precisely because we have this unconditional love that we find it so hard to cope with the challenges that parenting can bring. It's how we navigate these rough patches that matter.

That "joys" part of parenting is said a bit tongue in cheek! It is about the yin and yang of parenting!

Many parents don't know where to pitch their stance on parenting; because let's face it, when we first become parents, we have absolutely no previous experience at this role. it's not until we have finished parenting our children and when they are all grown up, that we know more about being a parent and what we should have done instead. Only problem is, by then your adult children will tell you that you are out-dated by the time they have their own children and that we don't do it like that anymore!

The journey to parenting is a learning curve. When your children become adults, you realize that if only you knew more when they were small, that your life and your children's life would have been a lot easier at the time and you would have done things differently.

Some parents are too soft whilst some others are too hard. Some care too much, whereas others don't care enough.

You can have the over-protective parents who are fiercely defensive and protective of their children or you can have parents who feel that once they become parents, that their life has completely stopped and that the only thing that matters in life, are the children. They no longer matter anymore.

They lose their identity as a person and become someone's mother or father instead of the person they once were. Their only conversation is about the children. They feel guilty if they have a night out by themselves without the children. In fact, if ever they do have a night out, their anxiety becomes so intense that they do not really enjoy the night out anyway.

Then there are the parents who due to their high anxiety about their children cannot trust anyone else with their child. Sadly, this anxiety can be passed on from generation to generation and that is not a legacy that you would want your children to inherit.

Many parents, very proudly tell me that they have never left their child (at the age of nine or ten) with anyone, since they were born... ... ... and why not?

I'm not saying that you should leave your children with just anyone! That is dangerous! But if you have people who are willing to help you and you believe in your heart that they would take good care of your children, and feel that you can trust them, then give it a go and see how you feel afterwards.

Don't allow anxiety to rule your life. You may find that your anxiety may calm down after you see that you are able to trust those who offer to help you. You do deserve a break some time! Remember what the saying says: **It takes a village to bring up a child.**

Nevertheless, this is your call! It is entirely up to you. it is your child, your choice and yours only to make! You choose how you want to parent your children.

You may find though that if you take good care of yourself that you can do a better job as a parent, and parenting your children become more rewarding. Being too soft, too hard, over-protective and over-anxious about your children do not do your children any favours. At the base of all these negative feelings is "Fear". Fear that you can pass on to your children.

In your zeal to over-protect your children, your children will not fail to pick up on your nervousness. Do not be so earnest about protecting them from physical harm, that you end up leaving them with the inheritance of your anxiety instead.

Relax! People have been having children since Adam and Eve. You are not the first parents on earth! This has been well tried and tested and if you do the right thing, your children will grow up, thanking you one day for the great job you did bringing them up as stable, independent adults in a calm and relaxed atmosphere.

Everything doesn't have to revolve around the children! You matter! Your relationship matters! Your family and friends matter too!

You are allowed "Me" time and adult time for adult conversations too, instead of "the usual brand of nappies" kind of conversation. It is perfectly okay to have dinner with your family and friends after you put the children to bed sometimes; or to have a special dinner between your partner and yourself from time to time, after the children's bedtime. The children are wonderful, and you adore them, which is wonderful, however, they do not have to dominate everything at everyone else's expense. You are allowed a break sometime and let the children understand that it's important for Mummy and Daddy to have their time too or time with their family and friends......and you can do it without guilt!

It is important to keep working on your relationship and not take each other for granted after you've had children. Some people keep a date night in the week to concentrate on their relationship, which is a great idea. If you make no effort towards each other, it is easy for your relationship to get into a rut and before you know it, you have grown apart. This is no way to have a quality relationship if you want your relationship to thrive. To communicate clearly and regularly with good eye contact is vital so that you both know where you are at and support each other.

Having a new baby can bring very stressful times for both mother and father. If you are not happy, very irritable, anxious, tearful, emotionally labile, have lost your joy of living, amongst other symptoms, you may be suffering from postnatal depression (PND). Postnatal depression affects one in seven women. However, this condition can affect both men and women. If that is the case please ask your doctor for help, as you may be going through very unnecessary and very distressing pain if you don't get the help that you need. There is no shame attached to this. PND can affect anyone, whether you are intelligent or not, rich or poor, working or not working. Don't let pride get in your way of asking for help. With help, you can recover and enjoy life once again. There is always the net to look for further information. Beyond Blue is a good website to visit.

The children do not have to be involved in everything unless you choose to of course. Some parents wouldn't have it any other way and that is fine too. For some, no matter how cute they are, it can be quite nice to relax with your partner alone or with your family or friends without the children demanding your constant attention. For others, it can be that having the children constantly with you from morning till you go to bed can be a good excuse to avoid dealing with other pertinent issues.

Remember, your children may have woken you up early and you have seen to their every need all day. It is perfectly normal to have a break from them for an evening or so. You will teach your children that the world doesn't revolve around them only, that you matter, and that other people are important too and they will thank you one day... ... or more to the point, you will thank "you" one day when you see your well-adjusted children! That is their first lesson in tolerance of others.

God gave you children, not to be a victim, but to take care of all their needs and your needs too, so that you can be a better parent. To be over-zealous, soon lets your little darlings know "who the significant ones in the family" are; as they very quickly realise and demand your attention all day long, because they "know" they matter and expect their needs to be met immediately!

You may find that you don't even have time to have lunch some days, because you are so busy catering to their every need. Well, your children are precious and important, but you are too. If you do not give yourself the same amount of importance you will not be able to maintain the pace and you can end up feeling resentful.

It will either affect you physically or mentally.

So, it's okay to say that "We will have a quiet time now, Mummy needs a little break". Even if your child or children no longer sleep during the day, they can stay in their bedroom and have an hour's "quiet time". You can train them to enjoy this little routine. It can be just enough for you to recharge your batteries and then you can start again, feeling more refreshed.

It is imperative for you to maintain a good self-esteem and self-worth. You cannot give your best and protect your self-worth, if you are too exhausted all the time and at the same time observe how well your friends are coping.

But, at the end of all of this, it is entirely up to you what you choose to do! It's your call! You are the parent! I am just sharing my experiences and knowledge with you.

In chapter one, we go back to how society was long ago and how parenting has evolved; what's lacking in yesterday's and today's parenting styles and about the use of praise.

Chapter two discusses how technology has changed us and the effects of technological advance, including how addictive technology can be.

Chapter three talks about what the Essentials are for a satisfactory childhood. There is a huge emphasis on being emotionally-available parents. Discipline as well as Taking Responsibilities, Exercise, Life-long good habits and Creative Play are discussed. Other topics mentioned are Instant Gratification versus Waiting; Social Interaction and Relationship, including Trust and The Entitled Generations are explored.

Chapter four asks "What can parents do?" and offers you many useful tips. It discusses "The Essentials for your Little-Adult-in-Training" as our children are apprentice-adults who one day will be fully fledged and fly the nest.

Chapter Five, Six and Seven discuss all the essential skills and teachings about "Preparing our children for a bright future" and what we need to teach them in their childhood to become accomplished adults with good self-respect, self-worth and self-esteem, who are kind, respect and accept self and others.

Chapter eight is about How it works and offers you very crucial parenting tips. Chapter nine to fourteen address some of the parenting challenges that can really stress parents out such as a Faddy eater, obesity or tantrums and much more and offer appropriate advice.

Chapter thirteen discusses the uncomfortable subject of bullying and what to do about it.

Chapter fourteen attacks the age-old debate of "To Smack or not to Smack".

Chapter fifteen addresses the important issue of your children's self-esteem and what to do about it.

Now, I want to spare a thought for all those parents who have lost their babies, child or children and send big hugs and love to all those who would have loved to be parents but sadly, haven't been able to. You are destined to be blessed in many other ways.

To be a parent is a huge privilege that we must be grateful for.

Well, I do hope that you will enjoy this book and that it gives you some guidance and relieves some of the anxieties that you may have about parenting and that it gives you the confidence of going ahead in the future feeling stronger as a parent, less anxious and more relaxed to love and parent your children.

Chapter One

Today's Society And How Parenting Has Evolved

You were born with the ability to change someone's life, don't ever waste it.

- Dale Partridge

How did we get here?

In Victorian times, parenting was much criticized for the severity with which children were treated; we now, have gone too far in the opposite direction, in allowing children to dictate what they want from a young age.

In the 21ˢᵗ Century, it is often reported that we are undergoing an epidemy of "entitled" children, even children and teenagers who are wild and uncontrollable that they terrorise their own parents, other children and some authority figures too. We even have toddlers who rule the household and render their parents into submission unless they get what they want.

We are having to face the fact that we live in a society where some parents are traumatized and are at a loss about how they can control their children. There are no winners here because, consequently, the children themselves, are experiencing devastating emotional ordeals due to the way that they were raised; unfortunately, as they get older they are having to face the difficult consequences of their actions, as they carry on the behaviours they have grown accustomed to.

If we want a different outcome, we need to go back to basics and help parents to teach their children right from wrong and stop them being so entitled to spare both parents and children pointless pain.

These outcomes are the result of their upbringing and the kind of parenting that they received. No one starts out thinking that they don't care if their children are entitled or have an awful childhood or behave badly. Very often the children's bad behaviour creep upon the parents little by little and finally gets to a point where parents are stuck and don't know how to cope with their children who are out of control. They are baffled about their children's behaviour and how to correct them or where to go for help. Suddenly, these parents find themselves in front of a "fait accompli."

Therefore, they either live in denial or just stumble in the dark and hope for the best or for a miracle; hence, the trauma that many of our young people are facing in today's communities.

The problem being is, that often we have "entitled parents" themselves bringing up "entitled children"! These scenarios frequently end up in disaster if they don't get the right help.

Unruly toddlers turn into unruly teenagers and unruly teenagers very often can come across a whole lot of trouble, such as being excluded from school, problems with the law or involved into drugs, alcohol abuse or other criminal activities, and may end up doing jail time, if nothing is done about their behaviour much earlier on.

It is vital that we do something to avoid this dreadful outcome on children, who, had they had the right parenting, would have followed quite a different path and alter their destiny for the better.

> *Parenting is the easiest thing in the world to have an opinion about, but the hardest thing in the world to do.*
>
> *- Matt Walsh*

The idea of this book is precisely to avoid these disastrous outcomes and to raise awareness. We need to educate parents, so that they can do a better job at giving their children a healthier and happier childhood, so that we can change these outcomes.

Parenting children doesn't mean doing everything for them or being completely selfless; but it means using a lot of common sense, kindness, love and affection, being emotionally-available, teaching them and doing what's right for them no matter what they want.

Some parents believe that they should treat their children as the "most important" members of the family. We all adore our children, but **everyone's** needs are as important as the other members of the family, including the mothers' needs!

Self-care is extremely important. If you take good care of yourself, it allows you then to take better care of others. If you don't take care of yourself, you will be able to cater to the needs of others for a while, but you won't be able to maintain it as you will eventually get sick or fall into self-pity or resentment.

So, to be a martyr or to be selfless is not a thing to be proud of!

Respecting yourself, your children and partner is something to be proud of! We all need to take care of ourselves to function properly and to be able to give better to others. When we are all spent out, we have nothing else left to give.

We can't give what we haven't got no matter how much we want to!

When children are treated as the most important members of the family, it leads to a generation of entitled children, as they are not used to consider the needs of anyone else, expecting having their needs met.

I like to think that every parent does their best with the knowledge that they have at the time. Sometimes ignorance can play a part when we don't parent our children right. In some cases, parents have their own issues and are unable to parent appropriately as they themselves have had poor parenting modelling and know no different; Or for some, it may be that the parents themselves were brought up with an attitude of entitlement which they unknowingly pass on to their children. Or for some others, it can just be life circumstances, for example, a single parent having to spend a lot of time working to make ends meet and not being physically present to attend to their child's psychological needs when they need them most. A child can mistakenly take their absence as them not being loved. Or it can just be that some teenagers are negatively influenced by the friends that they have and the environment that they live in.

Unfortunately, we now have a generation who can be often "unknowingly" selfish and ungrateful, think of their own pleasure first and their instant gratification due to the society in which they live. Of course, that is not to say that everyone of generation X, Y, or Millennials, fits this picture of our society. This is simply put, a generalization. The good side of these generations however, is that these younger generations are far more aware about the environment, recycling and saving the planet than previous generations ever were.

We are all influenced by the times we live in and the trends of that time.

Nevertheless, the fact is that this sense of entitlement and selfishness seem to be a modern disease that is quite contagious and is reaching epidemic proportions. We all need to take our responsibilities seriously and do something about it before this sickness spreads further and contaminates everyone.

Each generation has certain trends of behaviour which most young person love to adhere to, whether they are desirable or not, so that they can fit in with their peers. Our environment hugely influences us.

Whatever becomes familiar and seen daily becomes acceptable, good or bad.

Even if a parent does everything right, a child's contact with other children at school, clubs, the magazines they read, the articles they are exposed to on the net and social media, the parties they attend etc. make your child vulnerable to want to do what the others are doing so that they don't feel the odd one out, victimized or bullied by others.

Peer pressure is alive and well in every generation.

That is why as parents you need to remain vigilant and in-tune with your children.

Now, if what the majority is doing is appropriate behaviour and your child is copying them, we have no complaints. Unfortunately, bad behaviour seems to be far more contagious than good, especially selfishness, entitlement and ingratitude!

Children do things that they may not necessarily approve of, so that they can be like their friends and be liked by them. Although most children and adolescents say that they like their individuality, the majority want to be pretty much the same as their own crowd.

Just look at some young girls going out on a Saturday night, they are all dressed very similarly, hair done in similar fashion including makeup. Most young people do not want to stand out of their own crowd, although of course, there are always the exceptions to the rule. Somehow, the exceptions do not fit in with the "stereo-typical" youth and must have the confidence to stand out if that's what they want.

Unfortunately, selfishness, ingratitude and other negative behaviours are quite catching and spread very quickly amongst peer groups, especially with the help of social media, to the point that it becomes normal behaviour and they become unable to see that there is anything wrong with it. This is another reason why parents need to remain watchful over their children.

Mental Illness incidence

It is estimated that one in five Australian children (20%) are diagnosed with mental health difficulties. The most common mental illnesses are depressive (6%), anxiety (14%), and substance use disorder (5%).

The onset of mental illness is typically around mid-to-late adolescence and Australian youth (18-24) have the highest prevalence of mental illness than any other age group.

54% of people with mental illness do not access any treatment. This is made worse by delayed treatment due to serious problems in detection and accurate diagnosis. The proportion of people with mental illness accessing treatment is half that of people with physical disorders (The Black Dog Institute).

Approximately half of all serious mental health problems in adulthood starts before the children are 14 years old, although early onset of Bipolar disorder in childhood is rare. 11% of children are diagnosed with ADHD and many more children today are diagnosed with Oppositional Defiant Disorders, Asperger's syndrome or Autism than they were twenty years ago. This is not only because we have improved so much at diagnosing these conditions. There is also a high incidence of depression and suicide in teenagers and young adults, leaving families devastated. Many teenagers and young adults take away their own lives, many due to drug overdoses or cyber bullying.

This shows that we have an enormous responsibility as parents and as a society to ensure that our children are given the childhood that they merit so that they do not become a statistic of the future.

Your children's future is in your hands as their childhood is a good prediction of how successful or not, how happy or not that they will be in the future.

Why is this happening?

In Western society, in Victorian times, parents adopted the view that children were meant to be seen and not heard, as such ignoring the emotional needs and importance of the child.

Later, we had the generations of those who went through the first and second world wars. Sadly, these were times of great grief, stress and trauma; therefore, it was a matter of survival rather than being concerned about how we bring up our children, let alone being concerned about their emotional needs.

Coupled with these, there were also great concerns about the hundreds of thousands of children who died from infectious diseases, such as poliomyelitis, diphtheria, tuberculosis, tetanus, measles or whooping cough.

There were over one million cases of diphtheria diagnosed during the second world war, with huge numbers of children affected.

Parents were fortunate if their children grew up to become teenagers. It wasn't uncommon during these times for parents to have two or more children than they wanted as it was expected that they may lose a child or two or more to infectious diseases or some other disaster.

When smallpox was finally eradicated in 1979, it was estimated that it had already killed 300-500 million people in the 20th century.

Before the introduction of vaccination programs, 100,000 children a year still died due to measles, diphtheria, tetanus, whooping cough and other childhood infectious diseases. A fact that many anti-vaxxers have now conveniently forgotten. With the continued development of vaccinations and antibiotics, many more children survived; and the advancement in the medical fields helped our children to grow healthily and develop as strong adults.

During the days of the Traditionalists or Silent generation (born in 1945 and before), the mental, emotional or psychological needs of children were not even considered during these terrible times. Children grew up grateful that their parents somehow helped them to survive the wars and infectious diseases without having succumbed to some terrible calamity. However, even though there were such pain and misery during the wars and before, the children grew up respecting the older generations, because of the society they lived in at the time and the values that they received from their parents.

Despite all this, children were taught the very important principle of respecting their parents and elders.

Strangely enough, in those days there were far fewer bowling alleys, youth clubs, pool rooms or entertainment centres, if any, but I don't believe that teenagers stole cars, assaulted elderly pensioners to steal their money, killed others with a "coward punch" or stabbed others as frequently as they do nowadays, because they were "bored" and "had nothing to do", which is often the excuse we hear in today's world for the appalling behaviours of some young people.

So, how is it now that we have a lot of youth problems like these and often the excuse is, that there is no entertainment for the young and they do this because they are "bored!" and "have nothing to do"?

In the past, millions of adults and children struggled with the physical, psychological and emotional effects of the wars. Many were displaced supposedly for their protection and ended up being abused by the very adults who were supposed to take care of them. Sadly, psychological trauma is invisible, and all too often emotional pain is concealed and not expressed into words either, often leading to dysfunctional adults who carry their secret burden with great pain. That is, until recently when these "children" became adults themselves in their forties or fifties, having suffered for most of their lives, some very brave ones, have found their voice to denounce those who abused them at the time. This phenomenon has now evolved due to other courageous adults who have been brave enough to face their perpetrators and take them through the justice system.

Many of these same dysfunctional adults became the parents and role models of the next generation.

After the second world war, when the men came back home and there was peace again, the world suffered from the great depression as a result. It was a time for rebuilding.

Then came the post-war generations of the "baby boomers" (1946-1964).

For the first time in a long time, parents started to be able to appreciate and love their children for all that they were. However, many children grew up in less than ideal circumstances due to the after effects of the wars on their folks. Many men came back home suffering from post-traumatic stress disorder, some as amputees or suffering with shrapnel wounds.

Despite all this, children still learned to respect their parents and the older generation.

Let's not forget that in today's world, we have men and women who very bravely are doing their tour of duty in the Army, Air Force or in the Navy, many at great costs to themselves and their health and happiness and that of their families; this also means that there are many children who miss their mothers and fathers while they are busy working overseas, and these children are being parented by generous relatives.

When the "baby boomers" grew up and became parents themselves, they cared about the well-being of their parents as well as that of their children. This generation too was brought up to respect their seniors. Something that is no longer prevalent in today's generations. Why?

What is lacking in yesterday's and today's parenting styles?

Can it be that we have tip-toed too much around our children for fear of offending them, and damaging their self-esteem? Can it be that the balance of power is now reversed as the world has advanced in many areas of technology, medical and industrial fields, and the children are far more knowledgeable than the parents? Consequently, many of these children's needs take priority over everyone else's, they grow up with an inflated sense of self-worth and self-esteem and are not worried about putting themselves first before anyone else, unlike their parents and grandparents' generations.

They find it perfectly natural that their needs come first and cannot see anything wrong with it, as it has become the new norm, no matter what the circumstances are. Therefore, the respect for the older generation has gradually been eroded.

Whereas in past generations, however flawed parenting was, they had stricter boundaries and values such as respecting others, especially the older generation was never in question. Although the Baby Boomers' children didn't have the luxury that our children grow up with nowadays, their physical, psychological and emotional needs were considered more, albeit that it was still quite inadequate, than previous generations of children. Many still had poor childhoods due to their personal circumstances. Child abuse has always existed and sadly seems that it is likely to continue despite the efforts to stop it happening.

Hitting or "belting" children as a means of disciplining them was the order of the day at that time and prior to it. This practice was not considered criminal; in fact, parents believed that they were doing the right thing. Many believed that "if you spare the rod, you spoil the child". The problem is, where do we draw the line from it being a means of disciplining children to abusing them, when using corporal punishment?

When the children of the Baby Boomers grew up, they were given more, than other children ever had before them. This was not only because the world was developing and becoming more prosperous but also because we finally had the luxury of being able to truly appreciate the precious gift that our children really were, without having to worry about their survival through war or disease.

During that time, technology was developing in leaps and bounds.

Society by then, understood and made huge progress about the child's mental, emotional and psychological health, not only just about their physical health or their survival. We became more and more aware of the importance of children's self-esteem, emotional and psychological needs.

Then, came generation X (1965 to 1976) and generation Y or Millennials (1977 to 1995). These children were given even more materialistically than ever before. There comes a generation that have the latest trends or labels. Their parents want them to benefit from everything, as society becomes more and more affluent.

Consequently, many of them aspire to a lifestyle as good as their parents, but 20 to 30 years earlier than their parents did. Sadly, with this often comes this attitude of entitlement. They believe it's their right, not that it's a privilege. To achieve the lifestyle that they aspire to, both parents nearly almost must go out to work.

These generations are todays' parents. Someone coined the term "helicopter-parenting", which explains their over-protectiveness perfectly, as they do not see their children as separate from them, but as an extension of them, and as such can do no wrong. Their children are loved and praised continually, but somehow some seem to be far more dependent on their parents' help whether financial, emotional or practical than previous generations. Why?

There is a trend for many adult children to stay in their familial home far longer than previous generations did before them, some even in their late 20s and 30s and beyond. The financial benefit is one argument, but it's relative. Previous generations also had their financial issues but didn't depend on their parents to the extent that they do now. Can it be the issue of "expectations"?......

Some parents are quite happy and expect to keep their children under their roof for far longer and the new generations seem quite happy to live at home, have their independence without any responsibilities for the house and the financial burdens of paying bills for the house or utilities until they feel ready to move out.

Parents of grown up children have the expectations that it's quite acceptable to have their children stay with them for far longer than previous generations and the adult children cannot see an issue with it either. There is no judgement here! It is just an observation of how society has changed.

When children grow up and leave home, they are expected to be more independent and able to manage on their own. If they remain in the family home, they continue to depend on their parents and behave as "the child of the house", which doesn't encourage independence. They are unable to "spread their wings" and become autonomous all the time they live in the family home, when they are adults. Some even have a home-cooked meal presented to them, their laundry done, and they can borrow the family car if they need to go out. Why move out?

There are many who leave home and when things don't work out with their relationships, go back to their parents' home with their children in tow, often depending on the grandparents to support them practically, emotionally and often financially too.

I have worked with children and families for very many years but more recently it is more noticeable how many young children are being brought up by their grandparents, whilst the parents go out to work. Some grandparents may not have any choice but for some, it is almost expected, not realizing that although they are the grandparents, that they are ageing and as such do not have the energy that the younger generation enjoys, to cope for many hours on end to take care of toddlers or babysit sometimes until late at night. This reflects the times we live in and how things have evolved.

This is a gross generalisation, but one that is a recurrent issue very often discussed on television or in the media, which reflects what's going on in our society today.

Things have changed since the Baby Boomers generation, when their parents had an expectation that their children should look after them instead, as they get older.

With todays' generations, it seems that the coin has flipped. The adult children seem to have an expectation that their parents should help them look after their children.

This can be a huge commitment for grandparents, even though most want to help; however, it is up to the grandparents themselves to put boundaries and tell their adult children what they are able to cope with.

It is not cool to be a martyr.

The way that society has evolved, gives the impression that grandparents almost have a mandate to look after their grandchildren, like the previous generation expected their adult children to look after them as they got older. They don't have a mandate; they've had their time of child rearing. They do it because many of them want to, whereas some others don't have a choice.

Most grandparents do it out of love for their own adult children and their grandchildren and as such deserve their gratitude.

Often, the more giving the grandparents are, the more they can be taken for granted. It comes from the belief system that the adult children have about the society that they live in, their expectations and what they see is happening all around them.

The flip side of this coin is that many grandparents carry a lot of guilt if they are unable to help their children with their offsprings.

One of the problems may be, that the adult children have grown up with their parents and keep the memory of their parents as being stoic, ageless and capable of doing whatever that they have to; therefore, it comes naturally for them to turn to their parents when they need help with their own children. This "younger" image of their parents remains with them. Sadly, we all age!

They do not really see that their mother or father who was strong at 40 may not have that same power and energy in their sixties or seventies, as their image of their parents has not changed.

The younger generation explains it by saying "Oh but they love looking after their grandchildren!". Of course, they do! What grandparent doesn't love their grandchildren? However, the grandparents' needs and any afflictions that they may have at their age have to be considered as well as the safety of the children and all their needs.

Sadly, for a few others, the grandparents worry that if they dare complain, that there is the threat that the parents will not allow them to see the grandchildren.

The problem comes when the adult children can only see things from their own point of view.

It is however, the grandparents' responsibility, not their children's, to be honest and let their adult children know if things are getting too much for them, especially if it comes to the detriment of their health.

In other cases, if the grandparents are fit and well, and are

wanting to be more involved and they are happy to help with your children, it can be a wonderful thing for everyone and it's a win-win situation.

The grandparents can enjoy their grandchildren; the grandchildren can enjoy their grandparents' company and the adult children can get the help that they need.

If you do have older parents whom you are thinking of asking to commit to childminding regularly, be mindful that they may tire easily and remember to review that they are coping well with whatever commitment they may have made in their excitement and willingness to help, especially as the weeks turn into months and months turn into years.

Of course, the grandparents will tell you that the grandchildren are wonderful because they are to them, and that they love to take care of them as they no more want to age, just as you don't want them to either. They, too, want to keep the image that they are still young and capable.

No one, more than parents know how tiring it can be looking after young children, let alone when you are 30 to 40 years older and still doing it! This is not a disapproval or a judgement, it is just about raising awareness, and observing the change in society today.

You need to do what's right for you and for the grandparents and grandchildren.

Depending on your situation, you can give them the choice of coming over on their own terms to be a "grandparent" not a babysitter or childminder but to enjoy reading to the children or playing with them or taking them out for a walk in the park, without the "need to have to", because there is no one else to look after them.

If you have grandparents looking after your children, you know how hard it is to take time off from your work, right? then it is the same thing for the grandparents. It's just as hard for them to take a day off even when they really don't feel very well, knowing that you have your commitments. It's good to have a 'plan B' sorted out.

On the other hand, if your arrangements work for you both and both parties are happy and content with the situation, then that's great. Rejoice!

> *Remember that there are always exceptions to every rule! You may just be one of them! This is about raising awareness as most 70-year olds are managing one or more health problems.*

Generations X, Y and Millennials

Now, let's see, if we say that generations X, Y and the Millennials are selfish and entitled, although there are many factors involved, we also need to look at the generations before them that raised them and see how they were brought up and what was or wasn't expected from them and what environmental factors encouraged this selfishness if we want to change things.

Can it be that the previous generations were more tolerant and gave in more to these generations? Can it be that they believe that their children's generation is far more knowledgeable than they are and allowed their children to be the "boss"? or can it be that without the threat of wars or of deadly childhood illnesses we are more able to pamper our children and sometimes overdo it, and make them believe that the world revolves around them and their needs?

The thing is that there are many selfish and entitled but very lovely young parents nowadays, who have absolutely no idea that they are being selfish or entitled, because all of it is the norm for them. They know no other way. Their friends would probably behave in the same manner. That's the way they were raised.

They are just doing what their friends and others do and what they think is expected and approved of.

That is the way that our society has evolved.

Can it be that from the Baby Boomer era, where we no longer were threatened with wars and infectious diseases that families naturally became a lot smaller as parents didn't feel the need to have more children so that a couple of them survived? The threat of war was in the past and infectious diseases were reduced due to vaccinations. Therefore, parents can concentrate on the few that they have and can lavish all their love and affection on them rather than having to cope with eight, nine or even twelve children from previous generations, where probably no child got any attention?

Can it be that the world has become so affluent, that the next generations are achieving the same or better standards of living far earlier than their parents did? They expect more and want more even if they must struggle to get there. They watch television, movies, DVDs, videos and read magazines where the standard of living for some is very high and they expect it for themselves. But they want it NOW! Young people have a fascination with Hollywood, celebrities and their lives.

As a gross generalisation in middle Australia, it is not uncommon for households to have at least two cars, and if there are teenagers or adult children in the household, probably 4 or even 5 cars; many have 2 televisions if not more and a lifestyle. It is very common for households to come with swimming pools or spas; many of these households may have one or two 4-wheel drives, boat, caravan or motor home.

In a school near where we live, the car park is full of 4-wheel drives "p-platers", which belong to the students.

If these standards have become the norm today, many do not realize that this is far from being typical in other societies and their comfortable lifestyle can be taken for granted. It is a far cry from a village in Africa where adults and children must walk 6 miles to get some water, which is often, polluted!

This prosperity achieved at an early age often breeds selfishness and a sense of entitlement, as the younger generation struggle to keep up with their elevated standards of living. It becomes a case of the more we have the more we want, and if we must rely on our parents to achieve it, then they see nothing wrong with that.

I had the pleasure to meet a very lovely 21-year-old young lady this morning, who was charming and wise beyond her years. She expressed how her life is full of gratitude especially as she nearly passed away three times when she was younger; she said that she loved older people's company (of course, I liked her straight away!) as she believes that they are full of wisdom.

Like her, there are many others who are not dependent on their parents and who are not self-centred and selfish, and do not expect their parents to take care of their children most of the time or help them financially.

Nevertheless, it is a good question to personally ask yourself in all honesty: "Am I selfish? Do I expect more from my parents than I should? Do I have an attitude of entitlement?"

... ... Stop for a while! Think! If your answer to yourself in all honesty is loud and clear, then be happy with it or do something about it.

Inappropriate use of praise

Unfortunately, in the attempt to preserve the children's self-esteem, many parents give continuous praise to their children, to such a level that the children are constantly praised for whatever they may or may not do or achieve, in order that their self-esteem is not affected. For instance, if a ten-year-old does something very minor, then the world can hear enthusiastically how clever he is and how proud the parents are of him!

It is important to praise and give praise where praise is due but praise appropriately.

If your child has done something to help someone else or did well in his exams, then give them a lot of praise, don't over praise them when they failed their maths test. Don't make them feel like a failure either but help them to strive to be better; encourage them to do better next time without the finger of blame being pointed at them.

You can praise them often for the small things that they do to encourage behaviour modification. When a child is praised, it gives them good self-esteem and they are more likely to want to be praised again by behaving appropriately. Give good attention to the good behaviour.

Failure and Resilience

Nowadays when there's prize-giving, everyone receives a prize. They get a certificate for just turning up at a competition. They even no longer score some soccer matches in case children feel disappointed that they didn't score a goal. Sadly, no one has worked out that this kind of thinking is verging on the ridiculous! But more than that, at best, it can discourage those who work hard to achieve, if everyone who hasn't worked hard is rewarded in the same way as those who did; at worse it doesn't teach children to become resilient, to learn to problem-solve and to encourage them to strive to do their best and work harder to achieve their goals the next time. This way of bringing up children doesn't encourage resilience!

When we don't have resilience, any little mishap becomes a major problem. Unless we learn from our mistakes or failings, we don't learn to develop resilience. Mistakes fulfil a good function. When we are resilient, we can problem-solve and become resourceful.

The outcome of inappropriate use of praise results in entitled individuals.

Too much criticism is harmful to the child's self-esteem, but too much praise without any constructive criticism and inappropriate rewards, is as harmful to the child too. They become entitled.

It is only through doing something wrong that you can find out how to do it well the next time. That way you can learn how to deal with it when you must, on another occasion. It helps you to build resilience, which seems to be lacking in the way we raise children today.

We learn more through failure than when we get it right first time. Our mistakes serve a very good purpose.

When Thomas Edison was asked how he felt after having failed 10,000 times, when he was inventing the incandescent light, he replied that he hadn't failed but had found one more way how not to do it. The important lesson to learn here is that Edison never saw failure as a negative. He saw failure as just another "outcome", so it didn't discourage him. How many would have thrown in the towel after failing that many times? One could say that Thomas Edison was resilient! He never believed in failure. That's the sort of resilience that we need to teach our children.

If as parents you have a fear of failure, make sure that you do not pass on this fear to your children. Failure is just an outcome and we don't have to fear it. It is just a result, may be not the one they expected but nevertheless, it is a result. Next time your child can strive to get the result that they really want. If at first, they don't succeed, they must try, try again… ……until they succeed!

You need to help your children to see failure as an outcome rather than something negative to feel bad about and hurt their self-esteem. Instead teach your children to see failure as something to spur them on to do better next time without losing heart.

The problem some have today, when children are never told that there's a better way to do things, is that the first time that someone tells them that they have done something wrong, it can be crushing to the child, teenager or young adult, as they have never previously been told that they have ever done anything wrong. It can lead to a feeling of hopelessness and a desire to give up altogether.

Then, one day when they are all grown up and go to work, the world suddenly doesn't seem to keep praising them but downright criticizes them instead. They fall off their perch shocked that someone dares think that they are not perfect and has the nerve to reprimand or criticize them! They have no idea on how to react as they have not learnt to be resilient. They are crushed!

They have no previous life experiences to teach them how to react in such a situation. They can become disheartened, fall into despair or depression or they can rebel with anti-social behaviour.

Besides much has been invested materially by their parents to help them succeed and prosper. What they see, and feel is not what they expected, which leads to great disappointment. They believe that they are a priority and that their needs and wants come before any other. The problem with this way of thinking is that it leads to many relationships difficulties, whether personal or at work.

Children are little adults in training, whom, we aim to one day grow up and be self-sufficient, independent adults.

Childhood is a great time and a safe time for them to try things on, to make mistakes and to learn from them and to teach them how to do things better, so that as an adult they can be self-determining and cope with whatever life throws at them.

We want our children to grow up to be autonomous and able for them to cope on their own; to be self-sufficient, resilient and resourceful as adults.

A spirit of entitlement leads to a generation of self-centredness, selfishness and ingratitude.

A lack of care and concern for others, leads to a selfish society.

Unfortunately, even if you do not bring up your child in this way, they can be contaminated by other children who are, through social contact with others. We live in the days of social media, such as Facebook, Instagram, twitter etc. The parents' role is to pull them back and keep reminding them of the values that they want their children to live by.

When children become entitled, the basic rules of society are often forgotten, such as "please" and "thank you", and common politeness and good manners, because the world "does" revolve around them and their needs, as far as they are concerned.

The problem lies with the upbringing and the generation who brought them up.

With Generation X and the Millennials becoming parents, we now have parents who themselves, often feel entitled, who see their children as an extension of themselves, and as such can do no wrong.

Even though the problem lies with the parents who have allowed their children to become entitled, it is not to say, that once "the entitled" become adults, that they can keep blaming their parents for all their inadequacies. It is each person's job to educate and develop themselves.

Once an adult, the adult's shortcomings are their own responsibility.

As an adult, we can understand more complex concepts than we were able to, as a child. It is therefore our own responsibility to change things we do not like and have the courage to do something about.

The time to blame your parents for all your shortcomings is over. You are in charge of you now!

And if you are a parent, you are also in charge of your offsprings and have the responsibility to do your best for them.

Even if no one has taught you, we are all born with an innate imagination and intuition. Use it!

The same "entitled" parents are now giving more to their children at an even younger age. They often compensate with materialistic things for not spending time and effort with them, and they often rely on technology. Whatever, the child asks for, must be granted. The child is not to be thwarted or else they may have to deal with it!

So, how can the parents suddenly start to refuse to give them anything when they become teenagers and start to give them values instead? Impossible! We don't start to give our children values as they get older; they learn their values even before they start to understand and talk.

As teenagers, the parents lose their grip on them as they already feel entitled to do what they choose to when they choose to. Consequently, many parents have no authority over their teens, often resulting in entitled out of control teenagers.

> *Too much love never spoils children. Children becomes spoiled when we substitute "presents" for "presence".*
>
> *- Anthony Witham*

Today, it is very common for both parents to be in the work force, as we now have more university graduates of both genders, who want to be successful at their jobs to provide more materially and enjoy their lifestyle.

Many parents these days, must work long hours and even when they have finished work, still they must answer phone calls, texts or emails.

The guilt that these parents feel towards their children often interferes with how they would have disciplined their children if they had the time to care for their children's emotional needs better.

Many are in well paid jobs which believe that they also own their employees free time by expecting immediate answers to texts, emails or phone calls, when they are away from their work place at any time.

That's how our society has evolved!

CHAPTER TWO

How Technology Has Changed Us

Do not educate your child to be rich. Educate him to be happy. So, when he grows up, he'll know the value of things, not the price.

- Worldquotes.in

We are all very grateful for the monumental technological advance that we can all benefit from, but we must guard against allowing technology to take us over. Today, parents are so clued up on technology, that it becomes part of who they are, whether it is their phone, tablet, iPad, computer or games console. They feel that something is missing if they are not plugged into one of their electronic gadgets.

Children are greatly influenced by their environmental factors, and technology forms part of this influence.

Whatever you expose your children to, either environmentally or behaviourally, will have a huge influence on them when they are growing up.

Young babies are now introduced to iPads and iPhones to play with to keep them occupied. Technology becomes our babysitter of choice! The parents see it as a plus that their young children are so "clever" as to be able to handle the technology that they introduce to their child at such an early age.

How many young babies between one and three years old and beyond, have "their little index finger" ready to scroll down a technological page? Already they know what to do if they want to watch Peppa Pig or the Wiggles! If these babies are that easily hooked on technology, just imagine what the parents are like!

Today's children's challenges are greatly shaped by the environmental factors provided by their parents, albeit that their parents' intentions may be honourable in the first place, but the outcome can still be disastrous if the parents are not emotionally there to cater to their emotional needs as young children. Intentions do not matter, what matters is how your child is positively or negatively affected by their childhood experiences and what they are exposed to.

Intentions don't count when there is emotional damage occurring to your child.

The Effects of Technological Advance

With the advent of technology advancing at such an incredible pace in the last twenty years, we have technology at our fingertips for answers. None of us would want to go back before the age of technology, however, there are pitfalls to consider in the technological world that we live in.

The technology for mobile phones started in the 1940s but it wasn't until the mid-1980s that they became widely available. Initially mobile phones were cumbersome and weighed 1.1 kgs. (2.42lbs) and were not so advanced as they are now. Then, think how fast technology has advanced from what it was then, to the kind of iPhones or Smart phones or computers that are so easy available to the public now. On the other hand, technology has its drawbacks!

Technology is highly addictive.
To some it's their drug of choice!

We frequently become addicted to technology often without

even realizing it, as it becomes a generational norm, whether it is for personal use or work purposes. We become twitchy if we've forgotten our mobile phone at home or left it somewhere where it is not easily accessible! We feel something important is missing!

A latest research has even coined the name of this generation as: "The head down generation" as most people have their head down looking at their phones constantly, wherever they may be, in the train, the restaurant, crossing the road, on the beach, in fact, anywhere.

The iPads, tablets or mobile phones are given to the children to keep them quiet and act as an enjoyable childminder instead of bothering mum and dad. That way the children do not cause any embarrassment by screaming in public, and there are no parenting skills to be "judged on" by the public, leaving the parents free to focus on their own technology. So, as far as parents are concerned technology fulfils an important role.

Sadly, as the children grow up, they have been so used to have a phone or tablet available for their pleasure, the children themselves become addicted.

Meanwhile technology is taking the place of the parent. When parents and children are together and should be having interesting conversations to cultivate that parental-child bond, we no longer know how to converse with each other without having a phone each to relate to. Besides, this advanced technology is comparatively not very old in relative terms, do we know the side effects that all this technology and radiation has on young brains or young bodies?

To be able for these phones to function well, we need to have many phone masts which are mushrooming all around the cities, towns or villages.

What are the long-term effects of all these phone masts towers?

As much as being technologically savvy is a wonderful thing, some of our young children, some babies, are exposed to technology for hours on end to keep them occupied and leave the parents free to do what they want to do.

When technology takes the place of the parental role, parents become emotionally unavailable to their children.

> ***To be in your children's memories tomorrow,***
> ***you have to be in their lives today.***
>
> *- Barbara Johnson*

If the children are not in front of the television screen, they are in front of the iPad screen or tablet screen, or else the mobile phone screen or even some toys with electronic screens to entertain them or else the older ones can play an electronic game with a screen on their own play stations; Let's not forget some of the adults who themselves are addicted to their phones, computer games or some other electronic gadgets or Home Google (which I have to confess that I really enjoy!)

Looking down at a screen has become a huge part of the 21st century. When we are looking down, we are not opening ourselves to see the beauty around us or getting involved with what's going on, and we often miss out on the fresh air too.

Some parents are hooked on any technology, social media such as Facebook, Instagram, Twitter, snapchat, even Tinder, electronic games etc, so they cannot see the harm in introducing technology to their young ones early in their childhood. In fact, they believe that it's a good thing, as they see it as an advantage further on. The problem is that:

Children see their "electronically-hooked" parents as "emotionally-absent" parents.

They are so distracted by their phones, computers etc. that they do not see that caring for their children's needs doesn't only involve being physically present, they need to be emotionally-present to their needs too.

An electronic gadget cannot read and see to the emotional needs of children or replace a parent's face, lap, interaction and affection.

Some of these parents may be physically present, in the room, with them, but they are not fully present mentally and emotionally, when interacting with their children. They are preoccupied by their technology. The phone cannot make a bleeping noise without the urge of finding out what it is or who it is, which then more than likely requires an immediate answer.

The children may have a roof over their heads, warm clothes and food in their tummy but what they really need is their parents' love and interaction with them, affection and quality time. They want their parents to be aware of their emotional needs. As parents, you may give a lot materialistically and think that you are being great parents because you are generous to your children with material things. But that's not enough. Love, time and attention are more important.

What a child really thrives on is their parents' time, love and affection and their interactions with their mum and dad. A child's best teacher is their parent's face and their interactions with them.

> *Your children need your presence more than your presents.*
>
> *- Jesse Jackson*

How many times have you been in a restaurant where there is a family waiting for their food? In the meantime, instead of communicating with each other, each parent or child is busy on their respective phones, including the children playing games on their iPad, phone or some other technological game machine?

You cannot be fully present with your children if you have one eye on your phone, iPad or computer!

When you are not fully present with your children, you are not emotionally available to them.

This is a new phenomenon that previous generations haven't had to deal with as technology hadn't been so advanced previously.

When you are not emotionally there for your children, you cannot notice the subtle changes that can occur in them, warning you that something is going wrong with your young child or teenager.

When your child doesn't have your full attention, they are unable to share with you what is troubling them, and you may miss some obvious signs that all is not well with them if you are not tuned in to your child or adolescent.

An emotionally-absent parent may not notice the elusive changes that occur when their child starts to take drugs or when their teenager becomes withdrawn and depressed, has an eating disorder or is desperate because they are being physically bullied or cyber-bullied by others. Your child may not want to stress you by the way that they are feeling.

It's up to you to be sensitive to their needs and be there to notice these subtle changes and ask the appropriate questions.

Denial

On the other hand, some parents may be *"subconsciously aware"* of changes in their children but may choose to ignore it or live in denial; they may notice that their teenager is losing weight, that their pupils are pinpoint or dilated or that they look like they had been crying, but choose to ignore these parental intuitions and as they can't bear to think that if they acknowledge them... ... what then? It may be that all merry hell will be let loose for a while, that there will be many emotional dramas to cope with; hurt, anger, embarrassment! Difficult decisions to make! They cannot bear to think about it, so they play the game of not noticing anything!

The problem is that ignoring a problem doesn't make it go away! It just means that they will have to deal with far more problems further down the road, than if they had tackled it when they first noticed that something was wrong.

If you notice that something is wrong, deal with it there and then. It is far easier than to ignore it and having to deal with it when it has become a huge problem instead.

The way that society has evolved, has led to this devastating emotional state that our children suffer from today. Almost anything is acceptable. We have lowered our standards rather than raised them.

Many blame society, social media, the school, friends, other organisations, the television or newspapers etc. but after all this, the problem comes from:

The parents who brought them up!

As parents, you are given the gift of having children and are entrusted with their welfare. It isn't just your right to be able to have children, it is also your responsibility to give them the best of yourself that you can; and that doesn't mean what you can buy for them or give them in material goods. It means your time, your devotion to them, your love and warmth, your guidance and protection, and to be emotionally-tuned in to your children by giving them the best childhood that they deserve and by making the right decisions for them. It doesn't also mean that you need to wrap them in cotton wool and hover over them continually to over-protect them.

> **It is easier to build strong children than to repair broken men.**
>
> **- Frederick Douglass**

Socialisation of children starts with the parents when the child is still very young and going through different important developmental stages. By the age of three years old, a child has already acquired all their values. They have worked out what pleases you and what displeases you.

It is your job to give your children the best childhood that they can have, so that they can avoid having to go into therapy as an adult. That doesn't mean helicopter-parenting or stopping them from any experience that you would consider a little bit risky. Sometimes to love your children means to help them take calculated risks and it means to give them that freedom. Teach them how to keep safe and not to put themselves in harm's way without being over-protective of them.

Today's children's challenges are greatly influenced by the environmental impacts provided by parents. However, for some the outcome can be catastrophic if the parents are not emotionally there to cater to their emotional needs as young children or teenagers; or if they expose their children to stressful people or situations that can potentially be harmful to their children's physical, mental or emotional health.

What matters is how your child is positively or negatively affected by their childhood experiences.

Being physically present but emotionally unavailable is damaging to children.

The same digitally-distracted parents and some others who fall in the trap of overindulging their children to allow themselves their own time with their own "screen", allow the children to make their own rules, and as a result, the children rule the household!

Sadly, respect for the parents is almost the first thing that they disregard.

When the parents have no idea on how to handle their unruly children, somehow, they tend to go down to their level, rather than rise above it. Consequently, the parents are reduced to the state of arguing with their toddlers or teenagers as if they were on the same level as them.

The parents realise that the children are in fact in charge in the household but by then do not know how to change things. The household is chaotic, and the children become wild and throw massive tantrums if they can't get their own way. Therefore, as they believe that it would avoid confrontations, the parents give in; and the children learn: ... ... "if I cause chaos, scream and make everyone's life difficult... ...Yippee! I can get what I want!"

This is when we end up with situations like toddlers terrorising their parents, who don't have a clue on how to handle them, or teenagers who think that it's okay to punch their teacher and some even their parents! The children believe that they are the "Boss" and act as such. There is no reverence or respect for adults.

Sadly, these circumstances are what today's society must deal with. This situation didn't just happen overnight. It has been happening right the way through the child's growing years. The problem is that we demonize the children rather than see their demise.

It is not the children's problem only, it is a family problem; which is why we need to give help to the parents before we can see any improvement in the children's behaviour.

Discipline is not a word that some parents recognize. They believe that giving in to their children for an "easy life" is the best policy, because for the time being the children are contented, and they don't have to deal with yet another tantrum. However, it doesn't last and the children become little dictators who want their needs met, "NOW!" or else!

Some believe that if they reprimand their child that it would be damaging to their self-esteem. Wrong! You can reprimand your child in a respectful manner. You are their parent and it's your job to teach your children right from wrong. Children need to know for their own good, when they do something wrong and when they do something right.

Not correcting or disciplining your children is harmful to their self-esteem.

When children are never corrected for fear of damaging their self-esteem, they grow up with an overinflated ego and a sense of entitlement, which leads to arrogance, as their parents taught them that that they can never be wrong. If that's the case as a parent, you are not doing your job!

For some others the children quickly learn that if they create as much disturbance as they can, that their parents will let them have their own way.

In the household, the children rule, not the adults!

When children can oversee the household, they become very insecure. They realise that they don't know much but think that their parents don't know any better either. It teaches them not to trust adults as they believe that they don't know more than they do.

A household where the children are in charge is dysfunctional and only gets worse as the children grow older.

Lily Foyster

Technology has changed our world as today's parents are very often addicted to it; and as such have become emotionally unavailable to their children and now, are having to face the pitfalls of technology on their children and on themselves.

Chapter Three

What Are The Essentials For A Satisfactory Childhood?

In one school year a child spends 7800 hours at home and 900 hours at school. Which teacher should be the most accountable?

- Jim Trelease

What Are The Basics For A Happy Childhood?

1. Sleep

Children need to have adequate sleep as one of the prerequisites of a healthy childhood so that they can grow up with confidence.

I choose sleep as a number one prerequisite for a healthy childhood as no matter what else is right, when children do not have adequate or restful sleep they literally can't function properly.

Without adequate sleep, children can't learn properly, think clearly or behave appropriately. Their brain is foggy, and they must go to school already tired. If you can get their sleep right, then you can start to concentrate on the rest of your children's needs.

There are children who cannot sleep when they should, due to an over stimulation of their little brains with an overload of technology. As much as the technology keeps them quiet during the day, the nights become nightmarish to cope with, as the parents do not realize "why" their little brains are overstimulated and why their child won't sleep.

The parents go looking for solutions elsewhere, thinking that there must be a medical reason why their child doesn't sleep well. The child ends up having many medical tests for lactose-intolerance, reflux, infection etc. etc., and they all come back normal. That is because the child is normal!

What they need is good management and avoid the over-exposure of technology at their young age.

When children do not sleep well at night time, neither do the parents, who must continue their routine of early waking to attend work. This kind of scenario does not lead to a happy household, as parents become grumpy and over-tired due to lack of sleep themselves. It certainly does nothing to help their relationships and their efficiency at work! So, what do they do?....... of course, relax by entertaining themselves on their phones, social media, computer, television or some other electronic gadget to pass the time. Then, they too can't sleep even when the children are not bothering them.

Far too often children are allowed to stay up till all hours, playing games on their play stations, or playing on their computers or iPads or being occupied and lost in their mobile phones or watching television until late in the evenings, when they have school early the next day.

All these technological screens are very disruptive to teenagers and young children's sleep patterns.

The blue artificial light of the screens hits the back of the eyes, which then stimulates their brains at a time when they should be winding down to prepare for sleep. Consequently, the brain is excited at the wrong time and it's difficult for them to settle down and wind down.

So, when they eventually decide to sleep, their brains are far too stimulated to relax and sleep soundly and peacefully. The next day, it is hard for them to concentrate at school or are irritable at kindy, which is why adequate sleep is one of the fundamentals of a healthy childhood!

Due to lack of parental guidance these children get themselves into such a state that they are not able to react to what's happening around them in a rational manner, sometimes creating pandemonium around them, unless they get their way.

Lack of sleep affects and distorts our thinking, which in turn affects how we feel and how we behave.

As a parent your job is to ensure that your children have an adequate amount of sleep as part of a balanced childhood. The sleep training starts from the very beginning. Today, we are seeing increasing amounts of young children who suffer with inadequate sleep and who also have poor nutrition, as they dictate to their parents when they want to go to sleep and what they want to eat.

The after effects of the lack of sleep the next day, can escalade their disruptive behaviour and get them into trouble at school or create difficult behaviours at home for the pre-schoolers.

We all need a good night's sleep to repair and renew our bodies from the chemicals that have been used during the day. If we are deprived of sleep, this process cannot happen, and we feel tired and unwell the next day, making our coping facilities quite a challenge.

Other than sleep, diet and nutrition play a fundamental part of a child's growing up years.

2.   *Diet And Nutrition*

After ensuring that your child has an adequate amount of sleep, you now need to make sure that what they put in their bodies are the vital requirements to keep them healthy and give them the necessary energy that they require. So, the next essential element of a healthy childhood is the child's diet and nutrition.

There are many children who have a poor diet and inadequate nutrition. It may be due to a lack of knowledge of what constitutes a balanced diet and nutrition or due to lack of resources. If you want to know about something, it is up to you to go and research it and educate yourself; no one else is supposed to do this for you.

Some may be satisfied if the child has "something" to eat without being over-concerned if they happen to have a "big Mac" three or four times a week or chicken nuggets every night for an evening meal, so long as the child is not going to bed hungry.

Although there are lots of information about nutrition or diets in magazines and books, on television or the net, there may also be a false belief that good nutrition costs far too much money and that it isn't that important as the child "seems" alright.

If we realize that our brains and eyes are made up of 60% of Omega 3, then we also understand that if we do not feed our bodies with omega 3 our brain and eye health will suffer.

If our brains suffer then our thinking also suffers, leading to wrong decision-making and poor behaviour.

Omega 3 is mainly found in oily fish, such as salmon or mackerel, flaxseed oil, chia seeds, walnuts, fish roe or seafood. Other sources of Omega 3 are found in soy beans, spinach, squash, Brussels sprouts, Cauliflower, kale and Broccoli.

Nutrition plays an important role in a child's well-being and behaviour. Without the proper amount of nutrients and minerals, a child's brain doesn't function properly, and ultimately affects their behaviour. This interferes with their thinking process and mood. When the thinking process is impaired then the behaviour is also negatively affected.

Parents addicted to technology, believe in instant gratification, let alone their children who follow their parenting modelling. When they want something, they want it NOW! The problem is if you give in to what you know the child likes to eat, rather than what's important for them to have, you can end up giving them jam sandwiches for breakfast, lunch and dinner seven days a week.

Don't be shocked and think that it's exaggerated as I have known a four-year-old whose parents fed him on nothing else but jam sandwiches for over three and a half years! Whichever way you look at jam sandwiches, there are not a lot of nutrition in them, but a lot of sugar, which means that your child ends up depleted of many important nutrients for their growing bones and organs, such as iron, calcium, magnesium, selenium, potassium, vitamins, Omega 3 etc. etc. In fact, the sugar in the jam sandwiches negatively affects their behaviour and rot their teeth!

Encourage them to eat their fruits and vegetables daily instead. Your children need their daily dose of calcium for growing bones and teeth. They need iron, which is found in red meat, to stop them from getting anaemic, so that oxygen can be carried around their body for energy. They also need vitamins, and essential minerals such as selenium, potassium, calcium and magnesium in their diet to keep them healthy.

Research has shown that our brain has plasticity and is able to rewire itself through novel experiences and through our environment.

So, it is quite possible for children to be retrained, to be disciplined and to use their imagination and creativity if they are offered the opportunity of new experiences, to change their eating habits. However, children need emotionally-invested parents into their children's diet and nutritional values.

Parents need to take charge of their children's daily sleep routine and have a daily nutritional plan for their children's brain health and physical health and wire their brain effectively. For those parents who for some reason haven't been aware of their children's nutritional needs, the sooner they can be offered help to retrain their children, the better it will be for both parents, children, school and society.

However, pre-warned is pre-armed; the idea is not to allow children to get to the point that they need to be retrained. Pre-arming parents with children with parenting skills, which include what they feed their children can prevent health issues, difficult or damaging behaviours and long-term bad habits. Part of that training must include the daily essential dietary requirements of their children. However, for all to happen we need emotionally invested and emotionally available parents.

3. Children Need Emotionally-Available Parents

Sadly, the "techno-parenting-style" or lack of parenting, has negatively affected our children; It has helped towards wiring the children's brain in the wrong direction, contributing to today's youth's social problems and their own daily struggle. Technology-addicted parents result in emotionally absent parents who are ignorant of their children's emotional needs.

A phone or iPad cannot replace you as your child's care-taker, teacher or parent. They cannot show love and affection. They cannot humanly interact with your child. They cannot show emotions for your child to work out whether you're pleased with them or not, therefore you cannot help them raise their self-esteem. They do not have a voice to reassure your child, arms to hug and cuddle, a face to give a reassuring smile and lips to kiss their 'hurt' better with, and a lap to sit on.

Without the human love and interaction of you as a parent, your child is neglected, no matter how many expensive things you buy them.

Some parents may genuinely feel that they are not neglecting their children as the children have "all they need" ... ... that is except their parents' full attention.

If parents are not emotionally available to their children, then those children are neglected.

Parents need to understand that they can no longer be emotionally-absent or distracted with their technology, without their children paying the price for it in their emotional and physical health. In a recent survey, four out of twenty-one children wished that their mums would lose their phones.

Being emotionally-absent parents due to technology, is a new phenomenon that previous generations haven't had to face. It is something that the younger generations of parents are often not even aware of as they see it as the norm as everyone is doing it. They are completely unaware that it is even a problem which can devastate their children especially as they grow older.

What we need are more resources to educate and empower today's parents with skills so that they can be emotionally tuned-in and available to their children. They need to learn how to cope with their out of control children and for them to acquire new effective parenting skills, but most of all they need to understand the problems that being addicted to technology can cause.

When parents' perception changes as they acquire new skills, the children's behaviour also improves, much to the parents' amazement and delight. As the behaviour changes parents can appreciate the difference that an emotionally-available parent can make.

Their heart may be in the right place, but they got there either by default, ignorance or through their own addiction to their own screens or some other substance, because of the society they live in. Unfortunately, it is the children who pay the price in their childhood and beyond.

The problem is that these things creep up on them and before they know it, they are unable to live without their phone, social media, iPad etc. And when they look around them and see others doing the same thing, it becomes completely acceptable to them. Everyone's doing it! In fact, if you're not doing it, you are considered strange! Meanwhile many children are being brought up by parents who are emotionally-unavailable to their children; still the children grow up thinking that it's cool to be plugged in to technology most of the time.

Parents and children respond well to intervention. It is not hopeless, and society needs to be more aware that these parents need support and guide them towards accessing available resources, instead of criticizing them.

If we want to help the children, we need to help their parents first.

Very often as a parent, we tend to do what our parents did, as it is the only modelling most of us would have experienced during our growing up years, except for the technology which didn't exist in their days. So, many parents have no idea about the effects that their addiction to their technology can have on their children, as they do not believe that they have a problem.

Today's generations of children are being brought up by parents who are often emotionally unavailable. Life is busy, and they are technologically preoccupied through their work or their own preferences.

No matter how distracting parents are they need to understand that there's no substitute to good parenting!

If you want your children to have a happy childhood, you must invest the time and effort and you will reap the benefits as you witness your children bloom.

You reap what you sow.

Today's children are the casualties of their parents' addiction to technology. It affects their childhood resulting in social issues.

Children's childhood is the basis for them to transition into teenage and adult years. Their childhood will determine how successful or not they will be in the future.

Many adult emotional, psychological and mental issues start in childhood, too many due to poor parenting, which is why awareness of the importance of your children's childhood is crucial. Technology has added yet another dimension to children suffering from their difficult childhood.

Technology apart, another problem is that some of the parents are repeating the same poor modelling that they had when they were children, maybe thinking that they are doing the right thing, as they know no other examples of parenting, but in fact, are causing a lot of damage to their own children unintentionally, by not being emotionally available to them for different reasons. They repeat what they experienced in their childhood.

For instance, if their parents gave in to everything for a quiet life, they may do the same. As their children grow up, not only are they unruly and may be carrying out harmful behaviours, these children may mistakenly think that they do not have any parental guidance purely because their parents can't be bothered with them or just do not care enough about them as they are emotionally not there for them.

Drugs and alcohol also play a big part on some parent's availability to their children.

4. Discipline

Discipline is another essential element for a happy and balanced childhood. If parents are emotionally absent, they tend not to worry about their children's discipline as such.

All too often today's children do not have clearly defined boundaries and rules. They may also be getting mixed messages. "If mum says no, I'll ask Dad!"

As the rules, if there are any, are fuzzy, and there are no boundaries, the children are unsure of what they can or can't do; of what they can have or cannot have. Sometimes it may be okay to do some things and at other times, the same things are not acceptable.

Their morals leave to be desired; anything becomes acceptable. Some live with conflicting messages which leaves them in confusion. When children are confused, they act up, creating problem behaviours.

Children need clear boundaries and rules, and the love and affection of their emotionally-available parents for a satisfactory childhood. That's how parents can notice subtle changes in their children because they are tuned in to them.

Consequently, many children suffer the costs of an unbalanced childhood due to modern trends of technology, substance abuse, over-indulgence, selfishness, distracted parenting, no discipline, unruly behaviour, lack of respect and trust in the parents and other adults or figures of authority.

This scenario leads to disaster, which is what is often reported in today's news.

Children need clear rules that they understand and will respect and follow, knowing there are consequences to their actions. They need discipline and parents who invest in them emotionally.

Parents are the ultimate role models for the children. Every word, movement and action have an

> *effect. No other person or outside force has greater*
> *influence on a child than the parent.*
>
> *- Bob Keeshan*

Children who come from a background where there are clear limits and guidelines, know exactly what is allowed and what their parents will or will not allow them to do. Their moral code is clear.

There is no ambiguity and no mixed messages.

Along with those is an unwritten code of conduct that both parents and children understand and adhere to.

Both parents agree on the management of their children.

The children grow up with confidence unlike those who have an inadequate childhood who grow up with confusion and inconsistency.

The choice is down to the parents, which way they choose to discipline their children.

5. Taking Responsibilities

Children who have behavioural problems often have grown up with confusion and inconsistency and do not take responsibilities for their actions.

Children today are not encouraged to take responsibilities unlike those from previous generations who were encouraged to take too much responsibilities, perhaps far too young.

Children need to be taught, from a young age, that every action has a consequence; and that they are fully responsible for the consequences of their actions.

It's not always someone's else's problem to sort out, and not theirs. Children and teens need to learn that if "You do the crime, you also have to do the time" in other words, suffer the consequences of their actions.

Some learn this rule at great costs to themselves. Often when they are teenagers and in conflict with the law. They act according to how they feel in the moment and don't think about the implications of their actions until afterwards when it may be too late.

If they do not respect how their parents feel about their behaviour, then it is easy to misbehave and do things that other children with good parenting will not dare do, as they wouldn't want to hurt and upset their parents out of respect and a healthy fear of how their parents would react.

6. Exercise

For an adequate childhood encourage your children to exercise and keep in touch with nature.

Most people are happy when they are in touch with nature and can appreciate the beauty and fresh air around them. Many children have an inactive lifestyle as techno games are mostly indoor games. Consequently, the children are likely to spend a lot of time indoors, out of the fresh air.

Some children's early exposure to technology lead to generations, who would rather spend time with their mobile phones, their iPads or computers rather than be out in the fresh air.

Parents need to encourage children to enjoy nature and explore the outdoors, such as climbing trees or riding their bicycles. Regular trips to the park to kick a football or play with a Frisbee are fun and children and parents can enjoy the fresh air together as well as taking in some exercises. If you live near the sea, there often are very many scenic walks to appreciate or if you live near a park, you may be able to appreciate the greenery and perhaps the flowers and the vast space in which children and parents can enjoy together.

If you are a young mum who exercises at home or does yoga, encourage your toddlers or other children to do the exercises with you. As they grow up it will become part of their lives too. To keep them physically active, plan an obstacle course in the garden (safely). It can keep them busy and fit at the same time as valuing being in the open air.

Not only the children are not getting outdoors as often as they should, but over-use of technology leads to an inactive lifestyle for the parents too, contributing to the obesity problem that we are all experiencing today in children as well as in adults. Therefore, the exercise will not only benefit the children but the parents too, not only physically but also mentally.

There is nothing better than exercise to keep our mental health in good shape.

7. Life-Long Good Habits Start In Childhood

Life-long good habits often find their roots in childhood.

It is so important for parents to realize the role that exercise plays in the life of their children rather than allowing them to waste their time being inactive thinking they are not doing anyone any harm.

Problem is, they are doing themselves harm!

If exercise is part of their routine as children, they grow up with exercise as part of their life and will make time for it in their busy schedule when they are adults leading to life-long good habits.

These life-long habits also apply to other areas of children's childhood too, such as their sleep, diet and nutrition, behaviour, discipline, and the values that you impart to them. If they learn early on, to eat well, have adequate sleep, take plenty of exercises and behave appropriately and to respect self and others, these too, will form part of their life-long good habits. They will be on their way to a successful life and avoid the pitfalls of what we are experiencing in our communities today.

8. Creative Play

I think it's necessary to let kids get bored once in a while. That's how they learn to be creative.

- Kim Raver

Due to the availability of technology, both parents' and children' creativity and creative play can be easily forgotten. Cooking with the children, the use of play dough, imaginative or pretend play, building Lego or sand castles etc. are often a thing of the past. The issue here, is that if we do not make the time and effort for encouraging our children's creative play, it will not happen, and they will miss out.

If as a parent, you cannot see the importance of encouraging your children's creativity, you will not put in the time and effort and your children's imagination and creativity will be lacking.

To think creatively is of vital importance for children during their childhood to use the gift of their imagination and intuition to learn to problem-solve. The more they use their imagination to problem-solve, the better they get at it. The better they will be as an adult to problem-solve and to be independent.

Inspire your children to use their imagination in play. Rather than taking over their game and telling them what they should do because you are the adult and know better, follow their lead and ask them what they think they should do. You can help them to explore hypothetical situations, practice their problem-solving skills and decide what they can do, how to behave and learn from unexpected situations.

Often board games are very helpful to get their little brains working and thinking creatively, because at the end of the day, most children like to win the game and hate losing.

Children learn best through play.

When life throws us in a situation unknown to us, our creative side helps us to resolve problems, consequently increasing our problem-solving skills by making use of our imagination and our intuition.

Allow your children time to be bored and do not see it as a negative.

Make sure that all your children's time isn't completely organized by you. Don't feel that your children need to be occupied every minute of the day. Some children are constantly busy that they have no periods of unorganized time and there are others who participate in so many activities in the week that it leaves no room for them to experience any periods of boredom.

The problem with that, is, when these children come across a time that is not planned as such, they are bored and complain. They can't think creatively on how to organize their time. They have not been used to exercising their imagination to think for themselves and entertain themselves as their brains haven't had any practice at it. Instead of doing something constructive with that unstructured time, they waste it by whining or by participating in some negative behaviour that leads them into trouble.

Boredom stimulates our creative brain to develop. We tend to follow our imagination and our intuition. If we never have time to be bored, we can never know what we can be capable of.

Part of a healthy childhood is to experience times of boredom so that children can use their imagination to explore and discover new skills and get their brains thinking for themselves.

Our free time allows us to use our God-given gifts of intuition and imagination.

If your children's time is so fully occupied that they have no free time, then, they have no opportunity to use their imagination or their intuition, or to learn to problem-solve and explore possibilities by thinking for themselves. As such your children are missing out on the development of important life skills.

If children are not given regular free time, they tend to create havoc as a means of entertaining themselves when the opportunity presents itself, instead of using that time to be creative and inventive.

9. *Instant Gratification Versus Waiting*

The problem is that with the techno-games that have become such an important part of our children's childhood, they are constantly being rewarded with instant gratification every time and have learnt to expect satisfaction straight away in all areas of their lives too.

Technology including computer games can lead to addiction as it constantly triggers the Dopamine centre of the brain, (the pleasure centre), which is very much involved in addiction.

Consequently, children grow up not knowing what it means to wait for what they want; they expect to be gratified straight away. If they can't be, there's hell to pay! Later, as the children grow up into adults, they expect instant gratification as a matter of course, even if it means that the prize will be bigger and better had they waited.

Today's generations of parents come from the era of instant gratification too and often feel entitled themselves, so it is hard for them to be able to teach their own children about waiting for what they want and to stop them from being entitled, as many see nothing wrong with it.

Do not forget that there are exceptions to every rule! You may be that one!

So, we end up with a society who wants it NOW! They cannot imagine that waiting may mean that they may be rewarded with better in the long run. To be able to wait for something shows maturity. All too often instant gratification also means immaturity.

As their pleasure centre has been very active since they were very young, those children grow up into young adults who can easily be at risk of addiction to drugs, alcohol, smoking or gambling, as their Dopamine centre has been triggered on a regular basis for most of their lives.

So, teaching your children to wait for what they want is indeed a good thing.

10. Social Interaction And Relationships

Encouraging social interaction is very beneficial to growing children and forms part of their early socialization. It teaches them the social graces of our society, such as taking turns, sharing, good manners and how to relate to other children, adults and to those in authority.

Emotional and social interactions and relationships with others start to grow soon after birth.

Positive early care and experiences help children to form positive satisfying relationships and increase their skills and confidence in a social environment.

If a child is plugged into their technological screens a lot of the time, this emotional and social interactions and relationships with others suffer. Consequently, their social skills towards their friends and other adults are very lacking, which can be a big problem when the child is at school.

11. Trust

For a healthy childhood, a child needs to feel that they can trust the adults around them. For children to have a strong foundation for their development as a teenager and young adult, it is imperative for them to understand their own feelings and needs and those of others.

They are then able to start to develop trust towards others, especially in those who have a positive initial social interaction in their early childhood. This is of vital importance for children's social and emotional development as they grow up. This can only happen if they have parents who are in tune with them. If children have emotionally unavailable parents these stages of social and emotional development are hindered, and children are unable to trust the adults in their lives.

Throughout their school career and later, the people in charge of them will be adults. Other issues such as a lack of self-esteem, self-worth and poor self-confidence are the results of not being able to trust those around them, leaving children vulnerable during their teenage years and young adult life to behave in a way that is detrimental to them.

The Entitled Generations

Some of today's parents see their children as an extension of themselves and as such lavish praise, gifts and overindulge them, to such an extent, that their children consider these as normal and think that they are entitled to them.

The problem is that many of the parents themselves genuinely feel entitled, so they are unable to recognize the behavioural signs when their children are being entitled to correct them. It isn't until someone else points this out to the parents that they may be able to recognise this fact.

Many children are never told the word "NO"! Whatever they want they get! They grow up as entitled teenagers and young adults, who eventually have their own entitled children. They have a sense that the world owes them something and that somehow the world does revolve around them and firmly believe it and see nothing wrong with it. What's worse is, neither do the parents!

The children are considered as the most important people in the family. No! Everyone in the family is equally as important! Each member of the family has needs that have to be considered. To let your children, rule your household is dysfunctional.

When we allow our children to rule us, we are preparing them and us for a life of insecurity.

The result is the kind of society we have today.

Not only do our Children's emotional well-being suffer but we end up with entitled children who think that the world owes them!

Some of those parents now complain that their children are terrorising them, that they are out of control and that they can't cope with them, having no idea how it ever got this way.

No Child Is Ever Born Bad!

Our parenting Is crucial to their Behaviour. It is how we raise them that encourages good or bad behaviour.

Bad behaviour is something that they either learn through modelling or lash out due to fear, hurt and anxiety, or out of ignorance, immaturity and self-protection.

When children or teenagers are often misbehaving, it usually is the result of a deeper emotional or psychological issue.

Underneath their anger there is always hurt, fear and frustration.

Unfortunately, there is also a widespread use of drugs which some parents themselves could have unwittingly modelled in the first place. If children have been exposed to drugs, they would be desensitized to it and will not see anything wrong with using it.

Unfortunately, the use of drugs can trigger the worst anger, leading to appalling and dangerous behaviours, and can lead to mental illness.

Teachers see children as young as 5 years old, high at school the next day due to Marijuana smoke-filled houses. All this accounts for the difficulties that today's children encounter and for their "naughty" behaviour in or out of school.

Other extreme effects of entitled and emotionally-absent parenting are overwhelming, when looking at further health issues, such as over-eating as a means for overcompensating and filling the emotional hole; later there may be problems with the law, jail time or suicide.

It is imperative to avoid more children suffering these dreadful outcomes.

We all need to do what we can to help parents cope better with their children and help them understand the importance of being fully present with their children and lose the attitude of entitlement.

Nothing can replace the benefits of good parenting. Every child deserves a happy childhood, where they are loved and cared for, disciplined appropriately and have emotionally-available parents to meet all their needs.

That is not to say that every parent is entitled or emotionally-absent and that their children are experiencing serious difficulties. There are also the many wonderful parents who invest so much into their children to give them the best childhood that they can provide, and we thank God for them otherwise it would be anarchy!

However, this book is about raising awareness for others to follow in those parents' footsteps and help our next generation of children to have a more balanced and happy childhood, feel loved and see the world as a happy, friendly place where they respect themselves and others.

We can't be super-excited when the child is born and a few years later when they start to misbehave, decide to opt out of our parenting duties because it's too hard!

In fact, your parenting obligations do not suddenly stop when your child reaches the age of 18. Being a parent is for life. You may not be giving advice or telling them what to do, to an adult offspring, but

as their parent, you are there to love and support them throughout their life's journey. No! the job doesn't finish when they leave home! It finishes when you leave this planet!

When parents are expecting children, there is a lot of information given to them about the services available for help. We have medical centres, child and adolescents' health clinics and services, parenting classes etc. We can't plead ignorance! If not, there are plenty of information out there on the web or on those gadgets that many are addicted to.

If you don't know about something, ask, research, but do the right thing by your children, no matter what age they are.

It is your job to educate yourself.

As we all know technology is at our fingertips these days. Even if we took no notice then, information about child-rearing is everywhere. You can start with your general practitioner or child health nurse, for help to be sent in the right direction, let alone visiting Google and the net etc. There are numerous self-help books available on the subject.

It is imperative that children get good parenting in their childhood from parents who are emotionally available; not from parents who themselves are emotionally distracted and have a sense of entitlement.

It is essential for parents to realize that if you give your child all the material goods that they demand, that this does not equate to good parenting.

Materialistic things cannot replace the love and affection of a parent. Sometimes denying some things or making them wait for something can teach children a lot and goes a long way towards getting them to mature.

As a parent, you have a very important role to play.

The kind of parenting that your children receive has a serious repercussion not only on your children' future but on the next generation and on society and its future.

We are all responsible for tomorrow's generations and how they turn out, by how we parent our children today.

Chapter Four

So, What Can Parents Do?

If we want healthy, happy adults, we need to go back to basics and ensure that our children have a well-balanced, happy childhood. When we do that, the outcome leads to well-balanced, happy children and young adults and miraculous positive changes in others. During their childhood, you are training your children to one day become independent, well-adjusted and capable adults.

It is every child's right to have a happy and safe childhood where they are loved and nurtured.

Essentials For Your Little Adult-In-Training:

- **Be a parent, not a friend:**

Remember that your child has enough friends, they need you to be their parent that they can count on, not their friend.

- **Insecurity:**

Giving children too much lea-way makes them feel insecure. They need to have an adult in charge of them to make decisions for them that at their age they are unable to make for themselves. Just because a child says that he wants something, he should not necessarily be given it. He needs a responsible adult to decide what's right for him. When a child thinks that that the adults in their life do not know what they are doing, it leads them to insecurity.

- ### *Communication:*

How you communicate with your children matter. The tone of voice that you use is important so that your child understands you; for example, Your tone of voice should change when you are reading them a story or when you are encouraging them to eat their food, or when you are consoling them when they are scared or hurt or when you mean business when they are misbehaving. If your tone of voice doesn't change at all, your child may not understand what you mean and what pleases you and what displeases you, which creates confusion for them. For each of these scenarios, your tone of voice should have changed. So be aware of how you communicate with your child, otherwise, they can get mixed messages and feel insecure. When you give them instructions, be clear, concise and age appropriate.

- ### *Anger:*

Be aware not to take your anger out on your children as it's not their fault that you are angry. You may have unfinished business elsewhere! It is important for you to be able to control your emotions and not to lash out just because you are angry or unhappy. Do not slam doors, use bad language and behave in a way that you will disapprove from your children. If you are angry, put some space between you and your child, and… …. Breathe….. take deep breaths slowly. Calm down, then go back and deal with it. If your child is angry, acknowledge his feelings, tell him that you realize that he is very angry now, then encourage him to calm down so that you can help him.

- ### *Keep your adult worries away from your children:*

Be aware not to burden your children with adult worries or information that they can't cope with. Your financial issues or relationship issues should not be discussed with or in front of young children. Certainly, never bad-mouth the other parent in front of your children. All of this create an anxiety state in the children which have long-term repercussions.

- ***Rules and Boundaries:***

As a parent, your job is to set safe boundaries and clear rules. Have clearly defined guidelines. No ambiguity. You must have clear limits and guidance and stick by them. Your children need to know what those limits are and learn that they must adhere to them and you too need to play your part. Your child needs to know what is acceptable and what is not. The rule doesn't change with the days.

- ***Be consistent:***

You need to be consistent in what you say or do and not decide to change your mind at the drop of a hat. You will lose all credibility with your children. They will not believe what you say and won't be able to trust your word.

- ***Make a pact with your partner:***

Both parents need to be on the same page. You both need to be saying the same things no matter how much the children play up and manipulate you. Believe me they are programmed to test you! They're good at it!

- ***Consequences:***

Your children need to know that their actions have got consequences. They need to own their actions and understand that they must suffer the consequences of their actions, should they not obey the rules and that they will not get away with it, no matter what. This can be done in a gentle but firm manner.

- ***Be the adult in charge:***

As a parent, you decide what your children need; do not let them make decisions regarding their well-being or give them what they want when they want if it's not the right thing for them. You can have a discussion with them to point them in the right direction. A young child doesn't have the maturity to make complex decisions for himself or herself; that's why God created Parents! As they get a little older you can give them choices between two things to help them practice making decisions, but the main decisions regarding their well-being still are yours to take. For instance, just because your child doesn't want the nurse to put a needle into their skin and fears getting hurt, you wouldn't base your decision whether to vaccinate them or not on that, would you?

- ***It is their childhood:***
Your job is to give them a well-balanced childhood, that is to offer them a well-balanced lifestyle, with plenty of love and affection;

As previously stated make sure they have a well-balanced diet – plenty of fresh fruits and vegetables. Limit snacks and make them nutritious.

As a parent it is your job to ensure that your children have adequate sleep. Keep technology out of the bedroom. Have a set bedtime routine. Have a time when they go to bed and adhere by it. Be consistent about sleep as well as anything else. Encourage them to enjoy the outdoors and fresh air, which include some form of exercise outdoors.

- ***Imagination:***
Give them opportunities to be creative and have social interactions. If they show talent, do what you can to develop it.

- ***Free Time:***
Teach them to cope with unstructured times so that they can think creatively on how to organize themselves when there's time for them to be bored. That's when their genius comes out to play!

- ***Responsibilities:***
Teach them to take on age-appropriate responsibilities, by

making them responsible for some daily tasks from a young age. Teach them that everyone has responsibilities and that everyone needs to carry their weight. Don't keep them "a baby" because you don't want them to grow up too quickly or because it's your last child and you're not having any more babies, or because you are over-protective or over-controlling!

- ### *Don't be scared to say NO:*

Never be afraid to say NO to your child, if what they want is not good for them. Do it and do it without guilt! When you say NO with confidence, your child will get it! But if you apologize for saying NO they will realize that if they push you that you may change your mind, and you will cause yourself an unnecessary headache! They can keep nagging far longer that you can stand it!

- ### *Keep your word:*

Follow through with what you promised good or bad.
Most of all: Give them parents who are there for them emotionally.

- ### *Technology:*

Sorry to keep on with technology but it is a new development for parents to manage. Limit technology at lunch or dinner time. Use the time for family interactions and teach them good habits and table manners. Become very aware of your own technological habits.

- ### *Weekends:*

Make the week-ends as much technology-free as is feasible, and more family-oriented.

- ### *Values:*

Make sure your children get your good family values. Often family values are learnt during role-play and family board games. For example: That's when they learn that cheating is not acceptable... ...

unless cheating is one of your values??? Make time to have these interactions with your children.

- **Contribution:**

Teach your children to contribute to family life daily, from the time they are little. It starts with picking up their toys, to buttering their bread, to helping with the cooking, to putting the rubbish out, to unpacking the shopping, to cleaning up their room, to laying the table for dinner, to hanging the washing, to washing up or loading and unloading the dish washer or to whatever else you feel is reasonable considering the child's age. Encourage them to help, not only you, but others too if they are able to. Make them feel that everyone has a contribution to make to the family life, and not to expect anything in return, but to help with joy. However, you can praise them for what they do. A little praise goes a long way. Teach them to do things because they want to help. They form part of the household and everyone must contribute. No one gets away with doing nothing and let someone else do all the work! That way, you save yourself from being the victim that does it all!

- **Helping others:**

Encourage them to serve and help others from an early age and to give freely with a good heart and because they want to. It will come back to them in so many ways!

- **Gratitude:**

Encourage them to be grateful from a very early age. When your children develop an attitude of gratitude, anger and other negative emotions are very far away.

- **Independence:**

Encourage them to be independent. Your job as a parent is to encourage your children to learn to be independent so that they can stand on their own two feet when they grow up. It is unhealthy to encourage your children to keep depending on you.

- ### *If they need to go to camp or elsewhere:*

If they are old enough teach them to do their packing and unpacking of the things that they need to go away with. The next time it becomes their own responsibility. You can just supervise. Help them to be independent by making them carry their own backpack.

- ### *Lunch Boxes:*

As soon as they can, get them to start making their lunch box themselves, initially supervise them, then allow them that responsibility for themselves. If they forget it, they must suffer the consequences. Trust me, they won't forget again! ....and NO! you're not being cruel! You're teaching your children a very valuable lesson! They will not want to go hungry again....and no! they will not die if they miss out on their lunch once!

- ### *Take responsibility:*

Make sure that if they need sports, or dancing gear for school or clubs that they are in charge of packing them themselves. It is their responsibility to put their dirty clothes in the wash and to make sure that they are ready on the day that they need them. If they forget them, they must endure the consequences. Next time, they won't forget... and NO! it's not cruel! It's a big life lesson that they would have learnt!

- ### *Be age-appropriate:*

If they are old enough to do something, allow them to do it. Teach them the skills of how to do it rather than do it for them. Make their tasks age-appropriate.

> ***Give a man a fish and he will eat for one day.***
> ***Teach a man to fish and he will eat for life.***
>
> *- The Jesuits*

- ***Life Skills:***

Teach your children to fish, don't just give them a fish!

Teach them to be independent; don't do everything for them. Whether they are boys or girls teach them the life skills to be able to cope by themselves, such as cleaning, cooking, washing, ironing, shopping, DIY etc.

- ***Avoid being over-protective:***

Don't protect them from their failures but use them as a teaching tool. Mistakes are a good opportunity to learn from them. It will teach them how to overcome bigger challenges later in life. However, make sure that you make them feel safe about their blunders and that's it's okay to make mistakes. Often, that's how we learn. Teach them not to fear failure. It can be their friend.

- ***Teach them to wait:***

Rather than allow them each time to have instant gratification. Teach them to be able to wait for what they want. Waiting for what they want shows some maturity.

CHAPTER FIVE

Preparing Our Children
For A Bright Future

Part 1

It is not what you do for your children, but what
you have taught them to do for themselves, that will
make them successful human beings.

- Ann Landers

Often when we decide to become parents, there is so much to learn that we often don't learn about some vital knowledge and skills that would help us bring up healthy, happy and kind children who can go on and live an independent, quality life as an adult. Sometimes, some become parents not really because they chose to! If that is the case it can be a huge shock to the system and they have got a lot to come to terms with and quickly, if they want to give the child the best childhood they anticipate for them.

Frequently, parents research all about the pregnancy, all about the birth, and then learn all about how to make that baby survive without doing it any harm and helping him or her to grow strong; however, very often parents can neglect to teach their offsprings about some really important facts and skills for them to grow up respectful, courageous, grateful, happy, generous, compassionate, and successful human beings, who can make a difference in the world.

Don't worry, you will make mistakes…. We all do or have done! …. and as you read this, you are thinking of all the ways that your parents got things wrong, right? … … … But then again, were you the perfect son or daughter, without reproach?

The reason for that, is that none of us is perfect. So, we may as well forgive our parents and forgive ourselves too. If we do our best and educate ourselves on how to do a better job as a parent, then, hopefully we will not make dire mistakes, and we can give our children the best childhood that we are able to and can avoid our children painful emotional wounds that will follow them into adulthood.

This chapter is about the essential qualities that would enhance your children's childhood so that they can have a profound quality and fulfilling happy life.

It is best to start to teach your children from the time that they are still very small, for them to be able to naturally absorb the values that you want them to have. However, if you are reading this and you have an older child or a teenager, it is never too late to start to teach them good principles to help them have a better-quality life. It is better later than never!

They will be looking to you to model what you are teaching them; therefore, it is important to be congruent in what you say and what you do. Telling them to do as I say not as I do, because I'm your Mum or Dad won't work!

So, here are some essential qualities to teach your children:

I speak to everyone in the same way, whether he is the garbage man or the president of the University.

- Albert Einstein

Teach Respect And Boundaries

Respect is thinking about yourself and others in a positive way and acting in a way that shows you care about you and their welfare. Explain to your children what respect is as early as they can understand, which includes how a person feels about someone and how you treat him or her. Having respect for someone is that you have good thoughts about that person and how they behave including how you act towards them.

You cannot demand respect, you can only earn respect, by the way you behave.

Showing respect to someone means that you behave in a way that shows that you care about their feelings and well-being. Showing respect to others means that you treat them with courtesy and take their feelings into consideration.

Treating yourself with respect means treating yourself with consideration, and not do anything that can harm you physically, psychologically, mentally and emotionally.

Teach your children as early as possible to respect people older than themselves. Start with respecting you as their parents and you will not ever find yourself in a situation where your child threatens to do physical harm to you or to their teacher or disrespect you verbally when they get into their teenage years or even before, as often is the case these days.

Your children's training starts from the beginning and is on-going.

- If your child disrespects you, you cannot "demand" their respect, but you can ask them to "behave in a respectful manner", in the way that they conduct themselves and in their language. Do this straight away. Do not let them disrespect you half a dozen times then tell to act respectfully, because by then they have got used to being disrespectful and are less likely to obey.
- Focus on their behaviour not their feelings.

- Separate between your child's behaviour and who they are as a person.
- It works both ways: if you disrespect them and then ask them to respect you, you are fighting a losing battle!
- One mistake that we as parents often make is to take things personally and get carried away with the situation which often makes us overreact.
- Keep your focus on the issue in question and don't allow them to side tract you. They're good at that!
- When you overreact, you feel vulnerable and not happy with yourself. In the heat of the moment, you may use bad language or belittle others, which leaves you quite open to your children's criticisms. They are good at judging you! How can you reprimand them from over-reacting and using bad language when you do it yourself?
- If you want them to behave respectfully, it's vital for to conduct yourself respectfully too.
- Teach them that it isn't what happens to them that is the most important, but how they *react* to what's happens to them that really matters.
- Try not to take your child's side against another authority figure, as it will be easy for them to manipulate you and show you that they were right in the first place and that it's someone else's fault anyway! They will make you their partner in crime straight away and your child will not have learnt anything, but you may find yourself in hot water!
- Use praise to change behaviour. Praise good behaviour. Make sure that when they behave well, that you notice it and praise them for it. Children altogether respond well to praise. If you only notice their bad behaviour, they will not see the point of toeing the line, as you never notice when they are good.

Remember, your children are your harshest critics!

Unfortunately, in the times that we live in, there are many young people who do not show respect to their seniors. If they are on the train or bus and an older person, or a frail person or a pregnant lady, comes in and there are no seats available, make sure that they know that they must get up and offer their seat to one who needs it more than they do. It will be a very respectful thing to do. If they can help someone with a heavy burden, teach them to offer their help without having to be asked. You can hope that their example will influence their friends and others in a positive way too. If they have this basis while they are still young, it will carry on right throughout their life. This attitude and value of showing respect may stop your children from getting into trouble in their teenage years.

Many parents treat their children as their little "friend". You can behave in a friendly manner, but you are not their "friend"; you are their "parent!" Children need their mum and dad to be just that; their mum and dad, not their friend! When they are adults, if you want to go shopping together and be good friends, that will be great as by then your job of training them to be independent and good human beings would have been done!

Remember, your children have enough friends, what they need is a mother and father to love, respect and guide them during their growing years. They will only ever have one mother and one father throughout their lives. You cannot be replaced. You are there to love and lead them and make decisions for them as they are not old enough to make them for themselves and prepare them for adulthood.

Your children are a precious gift from God, lent to you to live under your guidance for only a few years. Before you know it, they will be flying the nest.

Do the best you can and give them the best childhood that you are able to give them. Time flies by very quickly! One minute, you're pregnant, the next they are starting primary school and you will blink and they are starting their secondary school and within no time at all, it seems, they've left home! ....and all this happened whilst you have been busy doing life, instead of savouring every moment you had with them as their parents, in those short few years! You need to learn to live in the moment and make good memories! Every day is an opportunity to make new unforgettable memories. Value your relationship with your children. The relationship you have with them as a child, will make it easier or not to come back to you when they've left home.

As you reflect, you will ask yourself, where has that time gone? So, make your parenting time with your children count; make this time enjoyable and give them the best childhood that you can possibly offer them.

Do the best you can to stop your children to look for therapy when they are adults.

When they get to eighteen or so, they may want to spread their wings and become independent and prepare themselves for adulthood. Some may go to university; others may want to go away travelling, others may want to live on their own or with friends. The fact is that they will fly the nest sooner or later…. Something else you will need to prepare yourself for! But most of all, your job is to prepare them to be able to live well independently.

If as a parent, you become their "friend", you now are on the same level as them. Children and teenagers often fall out with each other and can pick up their friendship again later, as they are on the same level, and it's okay. They have no awe factor or healthy fear towards their friends.

The problem when you are on the same level as your children, it becomes easy for them to disrespect you and treat you, as they would one of their friends. That really doesn't mean that they would disrespect their friends or that they should, but there is a certain "ease" that you have with your friends, that you would not have with your parents or someone in authority. There should be that natural respect that comes with talking to an adult.

Your children must know the difference between how they treat a friend and how they treat their parents. It is always useful for children and teenagers to have a "healthy" fear of their parents, so that parents can keep their parental authority over them, albeit in a loving and respectful manner, otherwise it will be easy for them to break your rules and they will not fear any consequences for their actions.

If your children do not have any concerns about breaking your rules and they know that you are powerless to enforce any rule over them, they can do whatever they want as they are not afraid of what will happen because you have no authority over them.

You need to have parental authority over your children for them to be able to respect you as a parent who loves them and has their best interest at heart so that they obey what you say, trust your judgement and guidance to do what's right for them.

Try and catch them from an early age or as soon as you detect that they are being disrespectful towards anyone and act on it straight away. You can plan and discuss how you will deal with them should they disrespect you. It will not come as a surprise and keep you wandering how you should react, when they do. If you do not act straight away, then the moment is passed, and you have lost the opportunity to teach them a lesson in respect. Make sure that your partner and you, both agree on whatever you decide. Children are great at playing one parent against the other or at the divide and conquer game.

Your children are little human beings and they are programmed to push the boundaries. You must be prepared for them.

Teach them basic social interactions from the start. If they know that there is a respectful way to interact with their parents and others from an early age, you stand a better chance of them being less disrespectful and making respect one of their main values in life. They will learn how to speak to their friends and how to speak with their parents. The way they speak with their friends may be acceptable to their friends, but they must know that they can't use that same tone with you.

If you allow your two-year-old to smack you, then why would you find it unacceptable if your fifteen-year-old smacks you?

We all learn by example. If you are not respectful of them when you interact with your children, do not be surprised when you are disrespected by them. You need to show respect to your children too as they are little human beings. Besides to make them value respect, you must behave in a respectful way towards yourself and towards others. If you can't show respect to others, why would you expect respect from your children?

> ***A lack of boundaries invites a lack of respect.***
>
> ### *- Pinterest*

When children grow up without boundaries, they become very insecure. Sometimes, parents believe that if they let the children do what they want, they will have an easier life; that is a fallacy!

Children NEED boundaries, almost from the very start. No boundaries also mean no respect. If children do not have strict boundaries, they become like little wild children or little dictators, expecting their way all the time. Parents need to agree how they handle and discipline their children and set limits and rules for their children and adhere to them.

Debbie Pincus suggests that "a boundary is the line you draw around yourself to define where you end and where your child begins". If you are a parent, you will know that parenting isn't an easy job. It's possibly the hardest job that you will ever do, but also the most rewarding! Children are programmed to test you and to push the boundaries as much as they can, to see how far they can push you. No matter how testing they are, it is vitally important to stay calm, loving and separate from your children, but all the same, stay strong and guide them and do what's right for them. Don't get carried away by the emotions of the moment; keep calm and stay separate. As your children grow up, start as you mean to go on when they are still little. Do not compare them to their sibling as each child is a unique individual who doesn't have to be like anyone else. No two children are the same. They all come with their own individual character and temperament.

You are in control of your emotions! In fact, we are all in control of our emotions, no matter what excuses we think we have.

A client of mine told me one day: "I couldn't help it, I was so angry, I kicked the cupboard and made a big hole in it!". And I asked her: If the Queen or the Prime Minister were to walk in at that same time, would you still have kicked the cupboard?" and the answer was: "Of course not!". So, if she can control herself when someone important is about to walk in, she also can control her emotions at other times too! It would take control for her to stop herself kicking the cupboard... .... Therefore, she was in control of her emotions. The fact is that it felt good in that moment to take her anger out on the cupboard door.... Because she could! But she knew what she was doing! It didn't just happen! Do not let your emotions highjack you! Stay in control of your emotions, no matter what!

If your children tell you that they hate you, you will just have to say that, that's very sad and that you still love them all the same, but that they still need to do their homework or their chores, whatever it is that they are complaining about! Don't get upset; it's all part of the job! Don't attach to those words as children know which button to press to get you going.

> **If you have never been hated by your child, you have never been a parent.**
>
> **- Bette Davis**

Do not take their insults personally. Rise above them! With children, tomorrow will be another story and they would have completely forgotten how much they hated you the day before!! The next day, they will be telling you how much they love you.

If you are having a conversation with someone and your children constantly interrupt and will not give up until you give them the attention, teach them to wait and make sure that you tell them that you are talking and will see to them soon after; teach them to say, "*Excuse me mummy*" or "*Excuse me Daddy*" and then deal with them *after* you have finished speaking. Do not stop your conversation to deal immediately with your child. You will not be helping your child.

Finish what you are saying first. Teach them patience and the art of waiting. Teaching your child that sometimes they must wait for what they want is important in this age of instant gratification, where they expect their needs to be attended to instantly. If you don't do this, you will become your children's slave! Besides it teaches them to be more mature by waiting, and to be polite.

Sometimes, a child may reprimand his sibling as if he were you; you need to tackle this and keep the boundaries well in place by letting him know that you are the parent and it's your job to deal with his sibling. At other times, they may overstep the mark and make you angry or embarrassed or even resentful. You need to prepare for these times. Reclaim your position of being in charge, stay calm and loving but firm, and remind them of the rules and that you are adhering to them.

If they do not show respect, there are consequences!

If you "lose it" because you are angry and have not been able to control your anger, you have already lost that battle and your child has won. Besides it is not a good example for your children to follow. That's good training for you too, to see how you can be in control of your emotions and behave respectfully. Be careful, that you are not taking out on your children some other unfinished emotional business elsewhere! Your child is not your emotional punch-bag! If that's the case, deal with whatever is bothering you, then deal with your child. If you can't do it alone, get some professional help. A Life Coach will help you sort this unfinished emotional business very quickly!

Children constantly watch their parents and guardians and survey their faces and facial expressions. Don't be surprised if they act out in the same manner.

Good enough for you! Good enough for them!

> *Kindness is the language that the deaf can hear*
> *and the blind can see.*
>
> *- Mark Twain*

Teach Kindness And Care For Others

Teaching your children respect doesn't start when they are 17 years old, it starts from the beginning. Equally, teaching them to be kind is an important quality and skill to build on and reinforce at all ages. It is important to cultivate kindness in your children from an early age and teach them to do something to help others whenever the opportunity presents itself.

Teach them to be happy to serve and to be kind to others. Don't let them expect to be served but see what they can do to help instead.

Learning to care and help others are important life skills that will stay with them all their lives and that they will pass on to their children eventually. It helps them to develop a community spirit and see the world in a positive way, which can only benefit them. It stops them from having an attitude of entitlement. Kindness is a very attractive quality that you can pass on to your children.

Someone once said:

The purpose of life is not to be happy. It is to be useful, to be honourable, to be compassionate, to have it make some difference that you have lived and lived well.

Teach your children to live well and make a difference in the world. Teach young children about doing a random act of kindness from time to time. They will learn how small acts of kindness help and please others far more than what the action meant for them to do it. Do not underestimate how these small acts of kindness help your children's self-esteem in the long run. They will feel good about themselves when they see how much their act of kindness meant to someone else. Teenagers can be taught bigger concepts grounded in scruples and honesty. These small acts of kindness are character building and will do your children far more good than you can ever imagine.

Studies even show that generosity and charitable gift-giving promotes longevity.

Remember that you are your children's role model. If you don't set the right example, they will not see the need to help others or to be kind either. If you don't care for others and tell them that they should; they will never believe you!

You may never know but your random acts of kindness may change lives in more ways than one. Giving to others and helping others is a great habit to get into and encourage your children to do the same. One of your charitable acts may just stop someone from taking their own life.

Getting involved with raising money for a good cause is a wonderful way for your children to learn about love, kindness, generosity and to become a team player with a community spirit, thinking about others and avoiding selfishness, which is all too common these days. If they are doing half a Marathon for a good cause, this will benefit them as much as the money will benefit the cause. They cannot help feeling good about what they are doing and have good self-esteem and self-image. This is in turn will keep them in touch with people of like-minds, which can't be a bad thing. Visiting an aged care facility once a month and offering an older lady or gentleman a bar of chocolate would probably make their year. Many of them do not have family visiting very often if at all.

We have lived in our house for the past 9 years and have had our wonderful 'little' (he is 6 foot something now!) neighbour, who is now 17 years old. He has put our bins out for collection every week for 9 years without ever having been asked to do so. He does it simply to help us as he has wonderful parents who are incredible role models! This simple act of kindness is of an enormous help to us. He puts the bins out in the morning on the day of collection and comes back in the evening to put them back again. An unbelievable kind, loving, compassionate and giving young man who is wise beyond his years, has a strong character with the most amazing future ahead of him. His generosity spills in all areas of his life, and many blessings await his future! He will reap what he sowed!

When you teach your children to be kind, it is not a waste of time and effort. Your children will reap the benefits all their lives. It will come back to them in more ways than one! Similarly, your children cannot reap what they don't sow, because you didn't teach them. If you have an elderly neighbour, find out what your young ones can do to help. You cannot imagine what a simple act of kindness can mean to your older neighbours. For all you know, your child may be the only contact that your older neighbours may see to talk to during that week. A simple act of kindness may be invaluable to them, but most of all, what it would have taught your child will be even more priceless. Something that will bless them all their lives. However, always ensure their safety first.

> ***Time does not heal everything, but acceptance will heal everything.***
>
> *- Pinterest*

Teach Your Children Acceptance And Tolerance

Teach your children from the time that they are still little to accept themselves just as they are, and to accept others just as they are too. Never allow them to say anything negative about themselves or others.

Teach them that the way they treat themselves is also the way that others will treat them.

If they don't treat themselves well, others won't either.

Self-denigrating talk steals their self-esteem from them. Stop it in the bud! For instance, if when they do something, they say that they are hopeless; it won't be long before others say: "Oh, Him! (or Her), they're hopeless!" On the other hand, if your child learns to say: "I don't know how to do this, but I'm really happy to try!". Your child will be seen and talked to in a positive light, which can only benefit them.

Accept that everyone comes with different gifts and talents and that some may be better at some things than others; but it still doesn't make one person better than the other.

To be able to teach your children about acceptance it starts first with the parents themselves. You cannot teach something that you cannot model yourself. Each time that you look at yourself in the mirror and say that you're fat, your hips are too large, your nose is too big etc. your children are watching and listening. When you don't accept yourself just as you are or have a negative opinion about how other people are, they will not fail to remember what you did or said.

What you say, how you react is imprinted into your child's mind in a flash, and they immediately form an opinion, good or bad, especially at times when you think that they can't see you or hear you. And when you say something negative about others, they will remember! And when you give them a talk about acceptance, they will see you as a hypocrite. If you don't believe for yourself what you are telling them to do, they will never believe you as they will see that you are not genuine; and don't expect them to do what you say.

On the other hand, if no matter how different others are from you and you show them kindness, tolerance and acceptance, your child will follow suit and will see it as natural to accept others no matter how different they are from them. They will find pleasure in diversity instead.

Acceptance is one of those lessons that is ongoing throughout their childhood and beyond. It is an important character trait of who you are. It forms part of your fundamental core values.

In your children's life, their parents are their most influential person. As they learn to accept themselves just as they are, teach them also to accept others just as they are. Everyone is an individual and it is their God-given right to be the person they are and choose to be. So as parents, we have the benefit of being able to influence our children to be kind and respectable to others, help them and accept others for who they are, whatever their differences may be. It teaches them tolerance of other people.

Every single person in the world is different, but we don't walk in their shoes, so we can't know what's going on in their lives and how they feel or think or what they are struggling with. We are all human beings on this planet with flesh and blood, a heart, with feelings and emotions! If we treat others differently, how would we like it if we were the ones being treated differently, just because we didn't fit their expectations of us? If you teach your children acceptance of themselves as well as acceptance of others, you are going some way towards making this world a better and open-minded place to be in, as it helps others to feel more accepted and integrated.

Your children's attitudes towards others can be infectious to those around them at school too.

Empathy, compassion and openness are the basic ingredients for acceptance.

Their examples may help other children to cultivate their sense of empathy and compassion, and in turn acceptance and tolerance towards others.

If every parent taught this to their children, there would be far less bullying in schools as acceptance and tolerance of others become the order of the day. Bullies always torment someone they think is "different and more vulnerable". If we can influence someone who has the potential to bully into accepting others and becoming more tolerant towards them, we will be going a long way, towards making school life a lot happier and safer for many children, sparing them from deep emotional scars that do not heal for very many years, if ever sometimes.

Acceptance helps your children to feel good about themselves and be more respectful towards others, therefore they are less likely to be the bullies themselves. Acceptance also encourages a sense of confidence.

Tolerance of others is crucial to better understanding, stops a judgmental attitude and allays unsubstantiated fear of those who are different from us. Most countries have a lot of different migrants these days, which means that many of us are different in our looks and customs than those of the host countries. If we learn to accept and tolerate diversity, it helps with letting people who have already suffered a lot in their lives to settle down in their new country, without feeling judged and less than, because they look different.

With tolerance as well as all with other values, it begins with the parents. If you are not tolerant towards your children, your family members and others, you are not qualified to teach your children about tolerance. If you judge others harshly, you're not qualified to teach anyone about tolerance. Sometimes, it is easy to be tolerant towards our own, but not so towards others. Challenge yourself and your attitudes and model tolerance to your children in your behaviour.

Children will never do as you tell them if you yourself do not do model it yourself. Be clear of how tolerant of others you are because your children will mirror what you do and what you say. They get all their values from you.

Your children will do more of what they see you do, than what you tell them to do.

If you model tolerance towards others, you will be teaching your children to be accepting and appreciate the differences in other people. Simply be kind and see it that we are all different but underneath it all, others are also human beings with real hearts, real lives and real feelings, real emotions, just like we are. They just happen to look different.

None of us choose where we get to be born. We are put on this planet by God and we are blessed if we are not the ones born in a war-torn country or in some other unhappy circumstances. So, if others come from a place less fortunate than us, the least we can do is to be kind to them and accept them for who they are and help where we can.

By teaching tolerance to your children, you will foster their self-esteem and you will help create a better world for future generations. Tolerance promotes openness and respect as well as empathy and compassion.

As our children are our future we pray that there will be peace in the world one day, if more people are accepting and understanding of their fellow man, open-minded and less fearful towards other people's practices and customs that are different from ours.

> *I believe the children are our future. Teach them well and let them lead the way. Show them all the beauty they possess inside.*
>
> **- Whitney Houston**

CHAPTER SIX

Preparing Our Children
For A Bright Future

Part 2

Empathy is about finding echoes of another person in yourself.

- Mohsin Hamid

Teach Empathy

According to Wikipedia, Empathy is the capacity to understand or feel what another person is experiencing from within the other person's frame of reference, i.e. the capacity to place oneself in another's position.

Being able to show empathy is a vital element of emotional intelligence.

Daniel Goleman says that 'empathy is the ability to understand others' emotions.... At a deeper level it is about defining, understanding, and reacting to the concerns and needs that underlie others' emotional responses and reactions. Empathy is the link between self and others. This is how human beings function and understand how others are experiencing things as if we were feeling it ourselves'.

Tim Minchin notes that 'empathy is a skill that "can be developed", and, as with most interpersonal skills, empathising (at some level) comes naturally to most people, and for others, they need to practice that skill daily, to improve it, but indeed it can be done'.

Teach your children the ability to stand in someone else's shoes from a young age. As empathy is a skill that can be taught, it will help those who find the skill of empathy natural and those who find it more difficult to learn how to empathise better. This will help them how to understand others. If you give them the gift of empathy it will carry them a long way. As children they may experience anger, sadness and loss in people they loved, and it can be quite confronting for them. If they have empathy they will be able to cope better with these feelings. Life goes full cycle of birth to death. Consequently, children will be part of the joy when babies are born but you can't protect them when one of their loved ones die, because they will be part of that too. Dying is a difficult fact of life that children must come to terms with and can't be protected from.

Younger children may not be able to name their emotions, as easily as the older ones. However, there are many children's books on the subject that they may relate to one of the characters to help them come to terms with their grief. Older children may have difficulty sorting out the intricate feelings, feel depressed but may not want to talk about it with their parents, which is why parents need to tune in to their children. This is especially hard when they lose someone of their own age as it makes their mortality very real.

If you have cultivated a close relationship with your children, encouraged them to be kind and show empathy since they were young, it may be easier for them to discuss how they feel with you, as they know that their parents are there and will empathise with them, no matter what.

> *I have found that if you love life, life will love you back.*
>
> *- Arthur Rubinstein*

Teach Love And Compassion

Teach your children to love and to be loving from the very start. You can use their dollies, teddies or bunnies to role play with when they are still little, by encouraging them to give them a cuddle or put a plaster on them if they are hurt.

When love is in their hearts, other negative feelings like anger or jealousy or resentment are not the natural feelings for them to experience. They will use love to extract more positivity in their lives. Love can only enhance their life and prepare them for meaningful relationships with those around them as they grow up.

The definition of compassion is "the ability to understand the emotional state of another person or oneself. Compassion is very often muddled with empathy. However, compassion is more than putting yourself into someone else's shoes, which describes empathy. Compassion has "the added factor of having a desire to improve or reduce the suffering of another".

Compassion carries a desire to do what we can to help ease the suffering of someone else.

Likewise, compassion helps you to have a different viewpoint on how you perceive others. For instance, instead of thinking that someone has hurt you because they are nasty, thoughtless and selfish, you may look further by trying to have an understanding for the person that if they did something to hurt you, there may have been other circumstances involved; in other words, compassion helps you to give others the benefit of the doubt. When you have compassion, you do not carry harmful feelings such as hate, anger, jealousy or bitterness in your heart, as whatever is in your heart will come out of your mouth.

Rather than assuming the worst, compassion helps you to see things from another perspective. It is thinking the best in others. Compassion motivates you to go out of your way to help someone else and show that you care. When you give help to someone in need, you do your best to encourage, reassure or even inspire them.

Showing compassion and giving kindness can really lift an

individual when they are experiencing a very difficult time. It can be enough to save someone's life or inspire in them a solution to a difficult problem that they were unable to resolve. If you teach your children about love and compassion from the start you are giving them a gift and skills that will help them to be a better person and help them make a difference in the world.

Research tells us that those who are compassionate tend to be happier than those who have no understanding for compassion. However, to feel empathy or compassion towards others, you need to begin with love in your heart.

> *If you want others to be happy, practice compassion. If you want to be happy, practice compassion.*
>
> *- Dalai Lama*

Like empathy studies show that compassion is a habit that can be cultivated.

When you have feelings of love and caring for others, it raises your own self-esteem, and helps you to feel better. When you feel better about yourself, you feel happier. Although we all want and need to be loved, but the "feeling" of feeling loving is what makes us feel good in ourselves.

If we can show and give compassion to others, we are not so harsh on ourselves either and can feel compassionate towards ourselves too when the need arises. If we are compassionate it becomes easier to forgive ourselves and show forgiveness to others. Give your children this very important and attainable gift.

> *Love all, trust a few, do wrong to none.*
>
> *- William Shakespeare*

Teach Trust And Faith

As with everything we want to teach our children, we have to be, what we are asking them to be and believe in. For us to teach our children to trust, we need to be trustworthy ourselves. Being trustworthy and teaching our children trustworthiness is a vital quality in which we need to invest in building in the lives of our children.

However, it cannot be a case of do as I say, not what I do! Your children will be the first to disapprove of this. They will remind you about incidents that you have tried to forget yourself. Consequently, it means that you must trust in yourself and behave in a trustworthy fashion on a day to day basis. None of us can be bothered by people that we don't trust, and least of all we wouldn't let them look after our children.

If we are to trust someone, we make sure that, that person, is honest, kind, reliable, credible, dependable and safe. How do we know that a person is trustworthy? First, it's by getting to know them. The Bible says that "if you are faithful in little things, you will be faithful in large ones. But if you are dishonest in little things, you won't be honest in larger responsibilities."

(Luke 16:10).

So, if you find you cannot trust someone in the small things that probably are not that important, you won't be able to trust them when it matters. It tells you a lot about that person's character.

Childhood is a great time to start teaching your children from a very young age and encourage them to learn to be trustworthy, in any small tasks that they do. Don't think, that it doesn't matter as it isn't important, because it does! You are building your children's character; however small they are.

Give your children small responsibilities to show that they are trustworthy and gradually give them more and more as they grow up, and don't forget to praise them each time. Any failure of their responsibilities is an opportunity for them to learn the importance of being trustworthy. Make the tasks age appropriate. Initially it may be to pick up their toys, and as they get older, it may be to make their beds and when they are a little older it may be to load and unload the dishwasher and may be as a teenager to mow the grass or clean the car. Those small tasks make them responsible for some things and they must follow through what they are asked to do, as well as responding well to someone in authority. You are also teaching them that no one has a free ride whilst one or two people in the household do all the work. If they do not do what they promised to do, you can use the incident to help them understand the importance of trustworthiness and keeping their word. When they say that they will do something, then they must do it.

At school, they will have to follow through with what the teacher asks of them. It teaches them discipline and respect for someone else other than their parents, in authority. This of course will be up to you parents to be patient and to train them well.

Make the training fun to encourage them, as children do not naturally want to do things that they find boring or not fun. Part and parcel of this training of course, means that, as they grow, they also learn that there are consequences to their choices and actions, and that means doing things that they do not find exciting. Whatever you teach them make it fun and show them how much it means to you when they do it!

However, there must be consequences for unmet tasks. You need to follow through with the consequences and be consistent in this. You cannot have consequences one week and then forget about it the next. Both parents need to be on the same page here too. If your children think that there will be no reprisals if they do not do what they are asked to, then there is absolutely no incentive in obeying their parents. It will be difficult for the children to respect what the parents say and do.

A system of rewards for good behaviour and a forfeit for bad behaviour is very useful to help them conform with what they are asked to do. For instance, no swimming on Saturday if the toys are not picked up and tidied away by the end of the day. However, you must follow through with it. Come hell or high water, you do not take them swimming no matter how much they complain! If by Saturday, you think that it wasn't that important anyway and take them swimming, do not expect them to do anything else that you ask them to do as they will not believe you anymore, and think that you will not follow through with what you say anyway. They won't trust your word!

When giving tasks take the opportunity to explain to them properly why it's important for them to do what they are asked and what trustworthiness is, not so much to make their parents happy, but "to follow through on the promises they made".

Don't assume that your children are naturally trustworthy. They are not! If they can get away with some things, they will give it their best shot! Children must learn, and you must teach them because children often like to push their boundaries as much as they can.

Have realistic expectations of your children. Don't expect more from them than they are able to give. Make their tasks age appropriate. This training will go on right through your children's childhood and beyond. Trustworthiness is very important whether at school or in the work place.

However, do not let it be something that will stress your children or make them experience disappointment after disappointment. Set them up to succeed initially and then build on that. If they think that they continually fail, it will foster a sense of hopelessness in them. Try to make it fun and praise them for their efforts, even if they fail.

Start off very small and gradually build up as they get older. Encourage your children to think of others around them and do what they can to help them and praise them accordingly.

Always reward good behaviour and try and ignore some poor behaviours if they make not a lot of difference. What I am saying here, is: pick your battles! Try not to conflict with them from morning till night! On the other hand, if you have told them that if a task isn't performed that there will be a consequence, then they must suffer the consequence. If you forget to check them, your children will stop worrying about fulfilling their tasks as they know that you will forget about it too.

When you teach your children to be trustworthy, and to understand the importance of integrity and honesty in their lives, you are also helping them to cope better with lots of other areas in their lives, as they will show maturity to be able to understand more concepts. They will have faith.

If you teach your children when to trust and when not to trust, it may serve them well and keep them out of danger when it is not safe to do so. Teach them that they cannot put their trust in just anyone, as unfortunately there are people with less than honourable intentions. Having a close relationship with your children helps them to be able to come to you if they are uncertain of any circumstances or situations. Always let them know that they can always come and discuss anything with you.

If you have taught your children to have trust and confidence in their parents, then you have also taught them the principle of faith.

> **Your faith can move mountain and your doubt**
> **can create them.**
>
> *- Greatisinme.com*

Faith is trust, an assurance in something or someone. Often when we talk about faith, we talk about our faith in God, in a Higher Power. Everyone is born with the capacity to trust and have faith in someone or something. The problem is what do we put our faith in? If you do have a faith in a Higher Power, then you owe it to your children to pass that on.

Research shows that those who have faith in a Higher Power tend to manage better in life and often enjoy more success in all areas of life. Their outlook on life is more positive as they trust that someone more powerful than them is looking out for them.

Encouraging faith in your children will give them confidence and peace of mind. To have faith and trust mean that they also reap the benefits of their positive thinking and their trust.

There is nothing like mistrust to make you anxious, resentful or unhappy.

Some people think that faith is something that you either have or you don't have it, or something that you are born with or that you can "catch" it, like the flu!

Others think that having faith may cramp their lifestyle as they may not be able to behave in the way that they want to when they want to. It is far cosier to have a lay in, in bed on Sunday morning than to have to get up and go to church! However, for someone who has a faith in God, it is something that they look forward to.

However, there is also the principle of having faith in oneself or in trusting our parents for example, we must have a faith that we can trust ourselves or that our parents won't let us down. Most of us have faith in something, but what can happen is that we can put our faith in the wrong things or the wrong beliefs. In that situation faith doesn't empower you or enhance your life. Many, put their faith in money and what it can do for them; they allow money to be their God! what happens if your luck changes and there is a lack of it or if you lose it all? Some things are worth far more than anything that money can buy!

The love of money is the root of all kinds of evils.

- 1 Timothy 6:10

Faith is an act of will. If from the beginning your children are secure in their family's beliefs, you will have children who are secure and know who they are and what they believe in.

Sometimes, people say that "the children will decide for themselves what they want to believe in when they are adults". There is a flaw with that kind of thinking because, if you bring your children up believing in nothing, your children will grow up with no knowledge of a Higher Power or need for spirituality, consequently, as adults they are less likely to be choosing something or someone or anything or anyone that they know nothing about! Besides you are the only model they've had, and if you had no belief in a Higher Power, then there a big chance that they will do the same.

If you have given your children a good basis of faith, they will make their choice when they become adults as they will know what it's all about and what they choose to believe in or change to something else if they choose to, having had a base of spirituality behind them.

It is well known that we are *Mind, Body and Spirit*. One doesn't work independently of the other two. Each affect the other.

If we feed our bodies to be healthy and feed our minds to be strong-minded, knowledgeable and think clearly, we also need to feed our spirits too.

In a study of 269 doctors, 99% of doctors believed that prayers heal and that miracles do happen. If we can give our children, the gift of encouraging the seed of faith in them we are helping them down a trustworthy path that can only help them especially when they are troubled later in life. When you cultivate the seed of faith in your children, it gives them peace of mind, confidence which lead to feelings of security.

> *Take the first step in faith. You don't have to see the whole staircase. Just take the first step.*
>
> *- Martin Luther King Jr.*

When one is secure, fear disappears, and your children feel more relaxed.

> *There isn't enough room in your mind for both worry and faith.*
>
> *- greatisinme.com*

> *Gratitude makes sense of our past, brings peace*
> *for today and creates a vision for tomorrow.*
>
> *- Melody Beattie*

Teach An Attitude Of Gratitude

Learning to approach life with the right attitude is a skill that we should all endeavour to master, as life is a skill in itself (*From, From Me to You, The Tapestry of Life and Its Secrets by Lily Foyster*).

Our attitude of approach to any situation determines whether we are happy or unhappy; it influences whether we are a winner or a loser, a success or a failure. It even decides whether we are sick or healthy, slim or fat, helpful or unhelpful, resourceful or unresourceful.

When we have a positive attitude, we are more likely to show gratitude. Teach your children to cultivate a positive attitude, as a positive attitude gives a positive outcome, whereas a negative attitude can only lead us to failure and self-pity. Negative thoughts take far more space in our brain than positive ones, so unless your child has an innate positive personality, it is essential to cultivate a positive way of thinking from the time they are still very small children.

From a positive attitude grows gratitude.

The world will react to your children by the way that they treat themselves and others. If they are positive the world will reflect that back to them. However, if they are negative, that is also what the world will reflect to them, often under the guise of being "realistic".

> *Life is 10% of what happens to me and 90% of*
> *how I react to it.*
>
> *- Charles Swindoll*

When your children or young adults have an attitude of gratitude, there is very little room for negative feelings such as anger, jealousy, bitterness, resentment, vengefulness, anxiety or depression to come into your children's lives. Therefore, less conflict into their lives, as a result your children are happier. With an attitude of gratitude, your children will not be tempted to flirt with unresourceful states such as jealousy, revenge or self-pity.

If the feelings are genuine, gratitude overcomes every negative feeling.

Teaching your children to develop an attitude of gratitude daily, is a wonderful gift that benefits your children and becomes a great habit as they mature into adulthood. It will keep paying lots and lots of dividends right through to their old age.

Remember that your children are little adults-in-training.

You are not bringing up children, but you are training them to be future self-reliant, trustworthy, resilient, kind, compassionate, empathetic, independent, grateful, loving adults with great self-esteem and preparing them for a successful life of contribution.

Whatever, you do with them when they are little children, will remain part of their childhood legacy forever.

Teach them gratitude and they will reap the benefits all their lives.

Can it be that you can avoid teenage problems if your children get into the habit of feeling gratitude from an early age?

During breakfast time, you can play a game and ask your children: "*What are we grateful for today?*", and as they get older, ask them to *name five things that they are grateful for today*. It can all happen whilst you are having breakfast without it taking any extra time in the day. It will prepare them for a positive day. Their thoughts of gratitude will be with them throughout the day. They will remember some of the things that they are grateful for and it will help them to react to their day in a more positive manner. Therefore, less problems with the school; less conflict in life.

Or you could give them a jar and every day they can to write on a small piece of paper what they are grateful for; fold the paper and put it in the jar. By the end of the year they can go back open the folded papers and see all the amazing things that they have been grateful for.

It will continue to foster their sense of gratitude, increased self-esteem and confidence in the world.

If they are given a gift, teach them to appreciate it no matter what it is, to show gratitude for a small gift just as much as for an expensive one. Make a point of encouraging them to call the person and thank them or else write a thank you note, but not by text. Nowadays, they are given so much that the lesser present may not be so appreciated as the ones of more value. Teach them that each has their value in gratitude and matters just as much, as they were given out of love with a good heart. This is good training for them and will stay with them all their life.

Far too often today, we have children with an attitude of entitlement. When they have an attitude of gratitude, they are less likely to have an attitude of entitlement. Those two attributes are opposite to one another.

Sadly, today's society is a "me" society, where the focus is "me", "myself", and "I". If you are a parent teaching your children to be grateful, don't make the mistake of thinking that you are not being observed. Little eyes observe everything, without a word being uttered; and little ears always hear what you don't want them to hear! Actions can speak a thousand words! You need to "walk your walk and talk your talk".

You cannot expect your children to have an attitude of gratitude if you yourself have an attitude of entitlement!

It is impossible to feel negative when your heart overflows with gratitude. The thing here is that you need to be sincere and feel the gratitude in your heart. If at first, you find that it doesn't come naturally, fake it until you make it! If you keep a journal of gratitude daily, whether you feel it or not, you will eventually believe what you are writing and will be able to genuinely express gratitude.

Gratitude unlocks the fullness of life. It turns denial into acceptance, chaos to order, confusion to

> *clarity. It can turn a meal into a feast, a house into a home, a stranger into a friend.*
>
> *- Melody Beattie*

If you are a busy parent who doesn't have much time for such things, decide to express your gratitude whilst you're brushing your teeth or having a shower and mean it so that your children can believe you. It takes no extra time! Or do it while driving the children to school. Make it a game between you and your children, but nevertheless, you are preparing them for a great day and for expressing their gratitude openly. The best way to keep your attitude of gratitude growing is to write it down. Keep a gratitude journal, where you can write down what you are grateful for each day and encourage your children to do the same when they can write. This way you can look back and see how many things you have expressed gratitude for. This can only bring positivity in your life and your family's life. When your children learn to write, give them a gratitude journal (i.e. a small exercise book) to fill in every day. It doesn't have to be an essay; it can be just a few words. When you develop an attitude of gratitude, you become more positive in your thinking. When you think more positively, you become more resourceful and see opportunities that you can never see when you are feeling and thinking negatively.

The world reacts to your attitude of approach in life. If you are grateful and positive, it helps you to be happier, more relaxed, have better relationships, and even feel healthier, and life is more fun. The good side to this, is that your attitude and your children's attitude will rub off on others and you can be a role model to others around you, enabling them to live a better-quality life too.

Give your children this gift. It can alter the course of their life and yours for the better.

Gratitude, courage, faith, determination, compassion and love – these are the emotions that we must nurture.

- Anthony Robbins

What does not kill you makes you stronger

- Friedrich Nietzsche

Teach Resilience

Parents have a very difficult job at home trying to teach and instil good values in their children, but at the same time, these children are subjected to ever-changing standards of morality by what they regularly see and by what they hear, which can be very confusing to children and adolescents.

Resilience is the "capacity to rise above difficult circumstances and not allow circumstances to get the better of us".

To be resilient is to recognize that we are human, with warts and all. It knows that we have flaws and accepts it because our world is hardly perfect. To be resilient helps us to overcome obstacles by carrying on with optimism and confidence.

Resilience is the difference between someone recovering well from a distressing experience and moving forward positively and another facing the same thing and giving up all together.

Children live what they see and all too often there is a great confusion in what is normal behaviour and what isn't. The language of children and young adults has deteriorated as they watch movies which use swear words so often that it becomes the norm for them. The language used in certain rapping songs are not the same as you would hear in church for instance.

At the risk of appearing to be a prude, but most would agree that the dress code is so loose now that anything is acceptable. Young girls can bear any parts of their bodies in such a way that years ago, they would have been called grossly indecent; but today, it has become the norm, and no one bats an eyelid at it. The short shorts have shrunk to the point that they barely cover much.

To young people growing up today, they cannot see that these standards are questionable as this is what they know and are most exposed to daily. They believe that they are keeping up with the fashion when they follow the same dress code as their friends and cannot understand why some people may see it as provocating and object to the way they present themselves to the world.

Whatever, we are exposed to regularly, becomes the norm for us.

Parents need to teach children to be resilient and help them cope and navigate the difficult terrain that they can experience as they are growing up, especially as things have changed so much and no one can say that all of it is going in the right direction. As much as the technological world has made huge progress, the social world seems to be more complicated.

Due to the continually changing standards of ethics and morality that becomes the norm for today's children, whose innocence can get them unwittingly into trouble, as they have no realisation that they may be in harm's way. Children need to be resilient so that they can overcome whatever difficulties that is thrown at them.

Your job as a parent is to shield your children from unforeseen problems that they may not see coming their way. However, protecting them is not enough and your children may very well fight against it too.

You need to educate them to keep themselves safe from unexpected difficult situations; teach them to problem-solve, to learn from their mistakes and to equip them to become resilient.

You can't shelter your children from every little hurt or upset. When you are over-protective, you do not allow them to learn from their mistakes or from their experiences. You stop them from learning how to problem-solve for themselves and how to build their resilience. They will expect their parents each time to come and sort their problems out for them instead of being able to do what they can do to solve them themselves.

Don't bring up a Prince or a Princess! Teach them to learn from what happens to them so that they can be robust and cope with what life throws at them. If something happens to them, do not over-panic. If you do, you will teach them that the world is unsafe out there and that will make them lose confidence and it will do nothing for their self-esteem.

When we don't have resilience any difficulties that we come across however small, becomes a disaster unsurmountable to deal with, and we cannot see how things can improve. So, each time that something goes wrong for the person who has no resilience, they behave as if the situation is hopeless and permanent and find it very difficult to cope and move on.

A young person who has resilience, will realize that they are going through a difficult time but that things will get better and that they will learn from the experience.

They realize that we all have good times and we all have bad times, but that the bad times do not last "forever".

Bad times always have a beginning, but they also have an end!
After the storm, the sun will shine again.
After the winter comes the spring. That's life!

Over-protecting our children, over-anxious parents, helicopter-parenting and the likes are not helpful to the children and does nothing to build their resilience.

Helping a child who experiences a difficult circumstance, being sensitive to their needs and at the same time helping them to develop resilience and offering them problem-solving skills, are far more helpful than taking over and removing the problem for them; as such, they will not learn how to deal with the situation if they find themselves in the same circumstances again.

> *Optimism is a happiness magnet. If you stay*
> *positive, good things and good people will be drawn*
> *to you.*
>
> *– Mary Lou Retton*

Teach Optimism, Enthusiasm And Confidence

Optimism is a mental attitude – a happy belief that the outcome of some specific endeavour or outcomes in general, will be good (Wikipedia). When we cultivate gratitude, positivity, resourcefulness, resilience, we also cultivate optimism.

When we are optimistic, we have hope and confidence of a positive outcome.

Help your children to see the world as a glass half-full rather than half-empty. If the world gives them lemons, the optimists will make lemonade; whereas the pessimists will be crying over the absence of oranges and won't know what to do with the lemons!

> *A pessimist sees the difficulty in every*
> *opportunity; an optimist sees the opportunity in*
> *every difficulty.*
>
> *- Winston Churchill*

Gratitude is closely related to optimism. Studies show us that grateful people are happier, receive more social support, are less stressed and are less depressed.

Research tells us that optimism has been proven to improve our immune system, prevent chronic disease and help people cope better with bad news.

Studies also report that optimists and pessimists approach problems differently, and their ability to cope successfully with adversity differs as a result.

Helping your children to be positive, enthusiastic, optimistic and glowing with confidence are great childhood gifts that you can and are able to give to them and which you and them will benefit from.

Studies also note that optimism is a skill that can be learned and cultivated. If your children are not naturally optimistic, you can teach them and cultivate it in them from a young age, so that it becomes their new way of thinking.

Optimistic people react to difficulties with a sense of confidence and high personal ability. They will not let their difficulties bring them down. An optimistic person will see their problems as temporary, limited in scope and manageable, whereas a pessimistic person can be panicked and think that it is the end of life for them or that the problem will continue long-term and will never go away. They cannot see past the problem, whereas the optimist may think that they may find a solution to their problem in the next few days… … … in the next few hours ……

As a parent you are in a privileged position to influence your children whatever age group they are at, to nurture a spirit of optimism.

> *Protect your enthusiasm from the negativity of others.*
>
> *- H. Jackson Brown Jr.*

Enthusiasm is "intense enjoyment, interest, or approval". As you have growing children, there are plenty of opportunities for you as a parent to develop your children's sense of enthusiasm in the world.

Again, as with a positive outlook, or being optimistic, enthusiasm encourages the child to find pleasure in his learning and reduces the risk of him being negative, pessimistic or unhappy.

Find things daily to boost your children's enthusiasm. It will become a habit after a while; then watch your children's self-confidence soar.

Confidence like the other traits above, must be nurtured and encouraged in children and will grow as they learn more skills in life. Confidence doesn't come naturally to some children, as some may be quite shy by nature. If they do something right, boost them and congratulate them and build their confidence little by little, brick by brick, so that they feel more confident to try new things. If they do applaud them; If they fail, teach them that failure is part of life; it is just an "outcome"; not the one they were expecting but nevertheless that's all it is, an outcome. It was great that they gave it a go. Encourage them to try again as they may get it right the next time.

You can learn a lot more when you fail at something than when you do everything right first time. Let's face it, no one gets everything right all the time! So, to fail sometimes is a good thing! That's how we learn!

> *Your attitude in life is everything. Failure is a*
> *bruise, not a tattoo.*
>
> *- John Sinclair*

Our face is the mirror that reflects to the world what is going on inside of us. Remember that your children are always scrutinising your face to know if they please or displease you. That's how they build up their values. So, if you are faking it, be aware that your children are watching! ... . Do a good job!

> **SELF-CONFIDENCE IS THE BEST OUTFIT,**
> **ROCK IT AND OWN IT.**
>
> *- Brainyquote.com*

Teach Emotional Intelligence Emotional Quotient (Eq)

> ***Any person capable of angering you becomes your master.***
>
> *- Epictetus*

Why do we need to teach our children about emotional Intelligence?

Emotional intelligence helps us not to take what others say personally and react with our uncontrolled feelings. It teaches us that if what the others say is valid that they can acknowledge it without losing face or feeling less than. However, if what the others say have no valid point, you do not take it on board. It is okay to acknowledge it as "one person's opinion" and not get offended by it. Everyone is entitled to their opinion, that's just what one person thinks, that's all; a million others may disagree with that one opinion! So, do not give power to an opinion that you do not agree with. Often other people's opinions hurt us because somehow, we believe deep down that what they said has some truth in it about us. That's why it's important to keep a healthy self-esteem and self-worth and not give weight to opinions that do not really matter. If something will still matter in 5 years' time, then give it a thought; however, if it won't matter, do not even give it the time of the day!

Teach your children not to get easily offended by what others say. It doesn't necessarily mean that what one person says, or thinks is 100% correct. It is not fact; it's just what one person thinks! Just like you may think differently from that person. Your opinion is as valid as the other person. You can just learn to accept that what they say is not what you think. Sometimes it's best to agree to disagree.

Emotional intelligence helps protect our children from unnecessary hurt and pain and teaches them how to deal with their emotions. It helps them to take into consideration the feelings of others and encourages self-reflection.

In addition, it helps children and adults to identify and express their thoughts and feelings and consider the thoughts and feelings of others. This leads to less selfishness, less hurt and bad behaviour in this very selfish world. Emotional intelligence teaches them about self-awareness and protects them emotionally.

You can start to teach them about emotional intelligence almost as soon as they can speak; you can teach them about identifying and communicating their feelings. If you talk openly with your children, they will feel safe and will be able to tell you how they feel and show empathy for others.

EQ can dramatically improve the quality of your children's and teenagers' lives, by teaching them how to recognize how they are feeling, where they're coming from, and learn how to deal with their feelings. If your children grow up with emotional intelligence, they are equipped with the most crucial skills for success in life. Rather than take things personally, they are equipped and prepared to see what is going on with someone else and react appropriately. Not everything has something to do with them.

Studies show that emotional Intelligence (or EQ) "predicts 54% of the variation in success (relationships, effectiveness, health, quality of life). Research also notes that "young people with high EQ earn higher grades, stay in school, and make healthier choices." When other children get confused with coping with their emotions, your children will have a clear advantage if they have been introduced to Emotional Intelligence from a young age and react appropriately.

So, the earlier you start to teach them about becoming emotionally savvy, the better. Further research has shown that having a high EQ has boosted social skills, productivity, academic performance, leadership skills and attention, while reducing anxiety, depression, and instances of bullying between students.

Any child can be picked on to be bullied by other children, but if you have equipped your children from a young age to identify and understand their feelings and emotions and those of others, they are less likely to be a target of the bullies. If your child doesn't react to the taunt of a bully, the bully will go a find some other victim to abuse instead of your child.

Daniel Goleman, (Mr EQ himself), believes that EQ matters more than IQ (Intelligent Quotient) and identifies 5 elements of EQ.

1. **SELF-AWARENESS**: Knowing our own emotions.
2. **SELF-REGULATION**: Being able to regulate and control how we react to our emotions.
3. **INTERNAL MOTIVATION**: Having a sense of what's important in life.
4. **EMPATHY**: Understanding the emotions of others.
5. **SOCIAL SKILLS**: Being able to build social connections.

As parents, it is your job to learn to handle your own emotions yourself, so that you can provide good teaching to your children. You can't ask your children to do what you can't do yourself. So, it all starts with you first, by using the above 5 elements, which fortunately can be taught at any age.

However, if you start with your children as early as they are able to understand, you will be giving your children an edge over others to be a success in all areas of their life.

We need to be honest and frank with ourselves, as we cannot change what we don't acknowledge. It is only then that we can change to be where we want to be.

Research on mindfulness tells us that a mindfulness practice can help reduce symptoms of stress, depression and anxiety in children. It can also increase gray matter density in regions of the brain involved in emotional regulation.

Yet, another study of adolescents found that yoga, which can increase mindfulness, helped students emotional regulation capacity.

Daniel Seigel, co-author of Parenting from the Inside out, teaches children to "name it to tame it." He encourages children to name their feelings so that they can get a hold on them and cope with them.

As parents, it will help your children when you are honest about your own feelings, naming them when you are angry, sad or fearful. Teach them that it is okay to feel all these feelings, as we are human, and we are expected to feel these emotions. Nobody is superhuman! Not even Superman! It's how we deal with our emotions that matters.

Arming your children with EQ is perhaps the largest skill set and predictor of their future success and happiness.

CHAPTER SEVEN

Preparing Our Children
For A Bright Future

PART 3

*Apologizing doesn't always mean you're wrong
and the other person is right. It means you value
your relationship more than your ego.*

- Brainyquotes.com

Teach Your Children To Say Sorry And Teach Them To Forgive

Some adults are never able to say this five-letter word,
"Sorry" … … Why? Because, they have never been taught to! Because
their mothers or fathers never said sorry, however wrong they were.
It's not something that their parents made a point of teaching them.
They believe that it is never their fault, it's always someone else's fault!
They grow up, with the thought and feelings that they are always
right, even when they know deep inside that they're wrong! How then,
can you teach your children to say "sorry" and to forgive?

The problem with that attitude is that it infiltrates many other
areas of life, such as your relationship with your intimate partner, your
relationship with your work colleagues, with your friends, in fact any

other relationship that you have, can be affected by the fact that you can't say "sorry" when you need to.

> **To forgive is to set a prisoner free and discover**
> **that the prisoner was you.**
>
> **- Lewis B. Smedes**

In your personal relationship with your partners, it can mean that not being able to say sorry, builds up resentment towards you and causes a lot of unnecessary frictions. Some have grown up, not only believing that they are never wrong, but that no one can tell them what to do either, which follows the same train of thought. "Don't tell me what to do! I'm never wrong! And as I'm never wrong why do I have to say sorry"?

I believe that someone who can meet someone else half way and say sorry even when they are not in the wrong is very attractive.

You may not be apologising for being wrong but to say sorry that you are having a disagreement shows a lot of emotional intelligence.

Some may show that they are sorry by buying flowers or gifts, but it never makes up for the fact that the three vital words: "I am sorry", are never actually spoken! Better still, it would be good to hear, if that is indeed the case: "I'm sorry, I was wrong; please forgive me". It will go an awful long way in making your children's relationships much better if they can learn this skill.

If you make the first move to apologize, you may find that most people will meet you half way and perhaps realize that they may have been partly to blame too. Therefore, it is a good way of resolving conflict quite quickly. It takes a small degree of humility to be able to say: "I'm sorry".

On the other hand, when you are clearly in the wrong and refuse to apologize, you show a great deal of arrogance. If that is what you are modelling to your children, you are preparing them for great pain when they are adults.

Arrogance is the camouflage of insecurity.

- Tim Fargo

Teach your children humility, not arrogance.

If from the start, you teach and encourage your children when they are in the wrong, to admit that they are wrong, teach them to say a sincere "sorry" to the other person; make sure that if they can repair the wrong that they've caused, and that they do it. However, if someone else says "sorry" to them teach them to be humble and gracious enough to say: "Thank you for saying sorry". Then, both can move on.

When your children are still small, you may need to sit with them and have a discussion about it and try and make your child see it from the other person's point of view and how they would feel if that had been them instead, if they are the one in the wrong.

There are always two sides to every story. Hear both sides of the story. They may have felt justified at the time. Then, rather than "blaming" them, teach them to recognize that someone has been hurt by their behaviour and that is wrong. The process of saying "sorry and forgive me" comes after this.

Teach them not jump to blaming someone straight away when something goes wrong. We are all only humans and as such we all make mistakes. Being kind to others goes a long way. People may do something wrong but we never know what's going on for that person at that time in their life.

Giving others the benefit of the doubt is really caring.

If they understand this, you can encourage empathy in your children and they are more likely by then to say a meaningful "sorry" because they've understood that by their actions, someone was hurt. Have you ever seen a child "spit" an apology, which looks like: "I'm not sorry at all but am forced to say sorry"? This kind of false apology is almost a lie as they don't mean what they say at all. Teach them to understand first and empathize, then train them to do the right thing.

As they improve with learning about empathy and compassion, they will more than likely be saying proper apologies by then.

If you are a parent who can't say "Sorry", think again!
Why then, should your child apologize?

We are our children's role models; if we don't say sorry, neither will they! Your children learn by your example.

Explain to your child that we all make mistakes. One mistake doesn't make anyone "bad". That's all it is: a mistake! However, this also forms part of your children's training to know right from wrong and it is the basis of our morality. It starts when your children are young; that way, they will not become adults with low self-esteem or with such arrogance that they are unable to apologize to anyone, however wrong they are.

As we are human beings, none of us are perfect! We all make mistakes! None of us can say that we are right all the time, which then means that sometimes we are wrong; when we are wrong, we need to acknowledge it and apologize for it.

The inability to forgive ourselves or those who have wronged us is often at the cause of a lot of people's pain, misery and ill health. Where there is unforgiveness there's always pain, resentment, hurt and anger lurking not very far away.

We can sometimes beat ourselves up so much and be unforgiving to ourselves for something we wish we hadn't said or done, or something we should have said and done. We can sometimes commit acts of omission as we can carry some acts of commission. However, beating ourselves up for it serves absolutely no purpose other than to harm us.

The first person we need to learn to forgive is actually ourselves.

Teach your children when they are still young to forgive the little things in life. When we can forgive small things, it then gets easier to forgive the bigger things.

Teach your children not to bear grudges. When they bear grudges, the only person that they are hurting is themselves. When they learn to forgive, there is a sense of relief that goes with forgiveness. Suddenly a big weight comes off the shoulders.

> *Forgive those who have injured you – not because they deserve your forgiveness, but because you can never be happy until you release your anger and grant forgiveness.*
>
> *- Jonathan Lockwood Huie*

Choose forgiveness in the little things in life; especially in the little things in life. As a parent, be careful when you are driving and the children are in the back; watch your language and your behaviour if someone cuts in in front of you! ... ... smile and choose to forgive and move on! We all make mistakes on the road at some point or another! None of us is perfect! The result will be that your blood pressure will not rise and you will not spoil your day by being stressed and eventually feel very bad as your children watched it all and heard it all! Again, you must walk your walk and talk your talk!

Forgiveness doesn't mean that you condone the bad action that someone has done to you, but that you are making a conscious choice of letting it go and not let it annoy, irritate or make you angry and upset.

Choose to let go of feeling bad. Choose to be free from any feelings that will spoil your day. It is within your power. You just need to be willing to let go and not invest yourself emotionally in negative feelings. Your children will follow your example.

The other person may not deserve your forgiveness but that has nothing to do with you forgiving them. When you forgive you make the conscious decision to forgive *for you*, so *YOU* can feel better. Forgiveness is not about the other person. It's about you choosing to let go and not sweat the small stuff.

Forgiveness is a gift you give to yourself.

Forgiveness doesn't mean that you necessarily have to have that person back in your life either or that you have to like them or have to associate with them.

Forgiveness means that you do not harbour bad feelings towards someone else and want the best for them, but it doesn't mean that you have to associate with them in any way if you don't want to.

Forgiveness means to be able to move on from where you were stuck. Nevertheless, forgiving doesn't mean that you have to be a "door matt"! It means that you choose to release the past but you don't have to put up with any old rubbish either. It is choosing to let go of all the hurt and the pain and you can breathe freely again.

Forgiving is a very selfish act. You forgive for your sake not for anyone else's benefit!

You forgive so that you can feel better and so that you can have peace of mind. Forgiving has nothing to do with anyone else but you, no matter what they did to you.

Forgiveness gives you peace of mind.

Nothing feels as good as peace of mind!

Teach your children to forgive while they can still do it, even tomorrow may be too late. In life everything is unpredictable! It's not because we are older that we die first. Anyone can go at any time if our turn has come, young or old. Only problem is, no one knows when it's our turn! So, let's not delay doing or not doing anything that we may regret tomorrow.

Tomorrow, isn't promised to any of us; Tomorrow is a gift, not an entitlement.

We can never go back on yesterday; tomorrow isn't yet here; all we have is the present. If we need to say sorry to someone, now is a good time! Living with unforgiveness in our hearts is very destructive. It encourages toxic chemicals to build up in your body and cause you many health problems.

If your children learn from the start that it is okay to forgive someone who has wronged them or forgive themselves if they have done something wrong, then as an adult, forgiveness will come naturally to them. Give your children that freedom.

In life, we get what we give out. If we can forgive others, others will forgive us too. Forgiveness brings healing and peace of mind.

Forgiveness is the best thing anyone can do to relieve unnecessary stress and anxiety in their life.

Humility is the solid foundation of all virtues.

- Confucius

Teach Your Children To Be Humble

The dictionary definition of humility says that "humility is marked by modesty, gentleness, diffidence, and a self-effacing attitude". The dictionaries can't help but contrast humility with arrogance and pride. Unfortunately, the society in which we live now is one which revels in pride and arrogance, especially in certain areas of life such as fashion, sports, the media, politics, or in the business world, particularly where money is concerned.

Recently, I asked a client of mind if he was humble? He was horrified and told me that he was absolutely not humble!!! I think that he thought that I was insulting him! As if it was a terrible thing to be humble (which, was the reason why I asked the question in the first place!........I already knew the answer!). Well, I had a lot of work to do!

Humility is often found in generous, kind individuals, who probably have a lot to be humble about. Usually, humble people are those who have a lot to brag about but choose not to.

Humility is often associated with people who have an attitude of gratitude. To be humble exudes charm to others.

Again, when you are teaching your children about anything, you need to be that person, who practices what he preaches! In this case, you need to model an attitude of humility, on a "consistent" basis. If this is you, your children can hear you bragging about how much money you make, far more than the neighbours, that you drive a far better car, have more exotic holidays and have a more expensive house! If that is what they are hearing on a regular basis, don't expect them to be humble!

The aim is to teach anything by example, which needs to be an everyday part of your lifestyle.

To be humble comes from a belief in something that gives us strength and confidence.

You need to teach your children to try their best in whatever they can do. Whatever, the outcome, so long as what they have done is their best, praise them for it. Give your children the confidence and humility to achieve the best they can.

As their parent, you are modelling to them that you value humility, and as such, your children will adopt humility as one of their main values. Help them to understand that you value them as your children not because of what they have achieved or not, but because you love them for who they are and that they are your children.

Do not demean your children because they are not showing humility. You cannot force or bully anyone into being humble. Lead by example.

Find some books on inspirational people, such as Mother Theresa who can bring humility to life for your children.

Teach your children to serve others rather than waiting to be served whenever possible.

Teach your children how to apply humility in everyday life. Practice with them until it becomes second nature to them.

If you teach your children about gratitude and forgiveness, learning to be humble can only blossom.

Begin each day with a decision to be happy

- happyjoblessguy.com

Teach Your Children About Having A Positive Outlook On Life

Encourage your children to be a ray of sunshine instead of a rainy day!

If we have a positive attitude, we are bound to think more positively and have more positive outcomes, and thrive on multiple levels that include the biological, psychological, mental, emotional, personal, relational and cultural scopes of life.

A positive attitude is essential if you want to teach your children to be optimistic and enthusiastic.

Not every child is blessed with a positive nature. It may depend on the kind of genetics that the child is born into. If your child has a tendency from the time that they are still young to be a little melancholic or morose, that is the child that you need to encourage more to be positive. Often, children react to what's going on around them. If they have a melancholic grandmother or an anxious parent, the child who has these people for role models is more likely to be more negative than positive.

Negativity is just a habit. It is something that is passed on in childhood and becomes a habit through life. Negativity can be passed on from generation to generation until someone is brave enough to say: No more!

If the grandparent is negative, they pass it on to the mother who has heard their negativity all their life and becomes negative as they don't know any other way; then, as a parent, they pass it onto their child, who in turn will pass it on to their child!!! Remember, if this is your background, stop that cycle right now! Teach yourself to be positive. Every time you have a negative thought, say the exact opposite to yourself. Refuse to entertain the negative thought. If you see the bad before you see the good as a habit, turn it around and start looking for the good before you can notice the bad.

Sadly, there are a whole lot of negative people in the world. Negative people always think of the worst-case scenarios to focus on. They often say that they are being "realistic". "Realistic" is another word for negativity. Sadly, for them it's true because it is their belief system and cannot see the positive, therefore they attract the negative like a magnet!

We are what our thought-life is. Think good and you will attract the good. Think bad and it will not fail to come to you.

In life we get more of what we focus on.

Whenever we focus on the negative, we are attracting negative events and experiences. On the other hand, the opposite is also true.

If we focus on the positive, we also are attracting more positivity in our life too.

What we think about we create in our world.

You, as parents have the privilege of being able to help your children to write their script on their life's slates. Let it be positive!

Successful people never waste valuable time focusing on negative outcomes. They concentrate on what can go right. What they focus on they create in their world.

We all create in our world what we focus on.

Help your children to be successful and live a quality life rather than a mediocre one. Help them to approach life with a positive and resourceful attitude. By teaching your children about being positive and cultivating enthusiasm and optimism in them, you are preparing them for a successful future.

> *Our thoughts and imaginations are the only limits to our possibilities.*
>
> *- Orison Swett Murden*

Nothing good comes out of a negative attitude.

Negativity blocks any opportunity that might otherwise have presented itself.

However, a positive attitude notices every opportunity in any difficult situation.

Remember, that you have to model this positive attitude in your own outlook towards anything and everything that you do or do not do if you want your children to have a positive attitude.

> *Make new friends, but keep the old; Those are silver, these are gold.*
>
> *- Joseph Parry*

Teach Your Children About Friends

Chances are if you have taught your children about EQ from the start, they will be wise in choosing who they make friends with. Unfortunately, we are all human and make mistakes.

Regrettably, sometimes, even when they know that some friends are not good for them, some children will make excuses for their friends or convince themselves and others, that they are wonderful human beings and there are no reasons not to keep them as friends. Sometimes, it's because they like these friends as they are charismatic and very popular. Other times, it may be due to peer pressure or your children may be scared of the repercussions of rejecting some popular friends. They may be afraid of bullying or they may be afraid of being ostracized themselves.

Before we can advise our children on their friends, we need to be aware ourselves of who our own friends are, whether they really are people we should be introducing to our children and if they are good role models too. So, a good frank look at our own friends is in order.

Proverbs 22 says:

"Tell me who your friends are, and I will tell you who you are and your future!".

Very true. Your friends have an enormous influence on you as they will have on your children. Many of us can't live without friends, but many can't live with them also! We won't hear a bad word said against them. Some would much rather have friends than family. Many would risk their lives for their friends.

Our friends can be the making of us, or they can be our biggest downfall. Friends are not the only influence over us, but their power over us is an incredible strength to be reckoned with.

Our friends can make us winners or they can make us losers. They can make us happy or they can make us sad. They can enhance our lives or they can help us destroy ours.

Friends are there in times of trouble or if they are not there, we soon learn who our real friends are. Some friends can be wonderful when everything is going great, but it is when we hit problems, that's when we soon learn if they are fair-weather friends or true friends.

For some who have very little family in this world or have no family in close proximity, our good friends fill the gap that family can't. These good friends are to be treasured. They are your family.

All too often we are not consciously aware of our friends' enormous influence over us. When we are good friends with someone, we, frequently end up seeing the world from their point of view. Their filters become our filters.

So, if you are to advise your children from the beginning about their friends, you need to do an inventory of your own friends and see whether they are suitable friends to introduce to your children.

So, think, do you trust your friends' values and beliefs?

Do you trust the decisions that they make? Are they a good influence on you? Are they a good influence on your children?

If your friends have a negative pattern of thinking or are of dubious character, the chance of you being influenced negatively by them is very high ... . and in turn your children.

When you are in close proximity of a negative behaviour and you see it regularly, it becomes the norm for you, even though you may make a thousand excuses for it.

When you start to copy a negative behaviour, there is nothing stopping you from acting in the manner, you once criticized. What's worse, is that by then, you will see nothing wrong with it. What started by shocking you is now so familiar that you are no longer able to be objective about it.

Remind yourself and your children that If you make friends with people of dubious character, you too will be judged by their standards and you and them will be tarred with the same brush!

People are judged by the company they keep, rightly or wrongly! That's just the way it is! If you are not proud of the company you keep, know that others may be saying the same things about you too.

If that is the case how can you be your children's guide to having good friendships?

Your children can learn from you, the values and beliefs that you look for in a good friend. They can learn about trust and trustworthiness, about honesty and integrity, about being reliable and generous, about tolerance and forgiveness and "about doing the right thing."

It is important to get their circle of friends right when they are still little children as you will not have much influence on them about their friends when they become teenagers. However, it is when they become teenagers that friends become even more influential on them. If they get into a bad crowd, you have to do what you need to do to keep them away from their bad influences on your teenager.

> **When anger rises, think of the consequences.**
>
> **- Confucius**

Teach Your Children About Consequences

I believe that it was Dr Phil who coined the phrase: "When you choose the behaviour, you choose the consequences." No truer thing has ever been said!

One of the most important life's lessons that you need to teach your children is that when they choose to behave in a certain way, they are also choosing the consequences of that behaviour. This life's lesson doesn't start at seventeen. It starts when they are toddlers.

As toddlers, it is important for your children to start understanding that if they misbehave, there will be consequences, such as Time-out for example.

If every time, your toddler plays with your television and you have asked him not to, you take him to the opposite corner of the room and hold him there firmly for a while, he will soon learn. First of all, he will not enjoy being restricted, but he will soon associate that the reason why he gets taken to the corner of the room and then held firmly, is because he is playing with the television which you have asked him not to do. So, unless he wants to keep being put in the opposite corner of the room and held firmly, he will just have to stop the behaviour of playing with the television. He will learn that touching the television means that the consequence is that he will be put in the opposite corner of the room and he will be restricted from moving. He is learning the consequence of his behaviour. You can start this as early as 18 months old. So, it's never too early to teach that life's lesson. Don't think that your toddler is going to get this lesson straight away, you may have to say it many, many times before the penny drops and eventually he'll get it! So, be patient and keep at it! It will be worth it.

Your children need to learn from a very young age to understand that each time they make a decision for a behaviour, they are also choosing their costs; when the children are in their teens, they will be well used to this rule if you started early. If they are offered cannabis or some other drug, they will know that there are serious consequences that goes with this behaviour. If they get into a fight and causes bodily harm to another or steals from another, they will know that they will have to suffer the serious consequences afterwards.

However, as a parent, it is your job, to keep reminding them throughout their childhood and teenage years that whatever behaviour they choose, that they are also choosing what will happen to them as a result of that behaviour. If they choose a good behaviour, there are good consequences, however, bad behaviours can carry serious consequences. This rule will stay the same all through their lives. It applies to you as well as to them or to anyone else.

Communication - the human connection – is the
key to personal and career success.

- Paul J. Meyer

Teach Good Communication

You may think that personal and career success do not apply to your children as they are still small, but like everything else in your child's training, it starts when they are still very young. The younger the better.

Teach your children to be able to communicate well with you and express what they are feeling. Teach them to use their words to describe what they want to say. Start when they are young so that they can identify different emotions that they are experiencing, so that they can learn to self-regulate.

If they are having a fit of temper, you can tell them that you understand that they are very angry at the moment, to help them identify how they are feeling. That way, they may be better able later to discuss with you, some of what they were feeling and their behaviours if they are not sure of them. Start this from the time they are still very young. But do not try to give long explanations to a toddler who is throwing a fit... .... he's upset, he wants what he wants and couldn't care less about any of your explanations. You can go into things later when all is calm but make your explanation age appropriate.

If you are not a great communicator, you need to learn more about it yourself and practice. Being a good communicator can only help you in all your relationships and especially with your children and your partner so that they do not receive conflicting messages from you to confuse them.

Being a poor communicator with yourself and with others can catapult you at the speed of light straight into the direction of pain.

Poor communication affects our levels of happiness.

Poor communication is often the cause of many misunderstandings and the subsequent grief that follows.

You may want to communicate one thing and your children may understand completely another thing. When you communicate something to someone, it is your duty to make sure that they have understood what you have just said to them. It is not their job to understand; it's down to you to make sure you communicated clearly and that your communication has been understood.

After you communicate with them, you can paraphrase what you just said to clarify things with them; you can say: "So, we talked about... ... .is that what you understood?" or you could ask them questions about what you just discussed to see whether they have really grasp what you have said to them. This will teach them to be clearer in their communication with you and others too as they grow up. Or you could say: "Let's see if I got this right! You said ... ...Is that right?" That way, there will be no misunderstanding from the start and your children will know where they stand with you. There will be no mixed messages.

For any relationship to flourish, we need to be good communicators.

Success in any relationship depends on the quality of our communication.

The key to any relationship, whether with ourselves or with others, is to be able to state clearly what we want and what we need and to understand what others want and need.

Good communications produce good relationships. So, if you start from the time your children are young, it will improve your relationship with your children and with your spouse. As your children grow up life will be easier for them as they are better able to express their needs and wants clearly and understand other people's needs and wants too.

Like everything else in life, you get back what you give out.

Put in little effort, you will get little back; but if you put in a lot of effort, you will be rewarded by what you put in.

Initiative is doing the right thing without being told.

- Victor Hugo

Do The Right Thing And Do Not Compare.

Teach your children to always "do the right thing." It may be that they have to follow their intuition in what "the right thing" is or it may be what the majority considers to be the right thing. If it feels right it's probably right; if it's feels uneasy, it's probably not the right thing to do.

If you have taught your children about integrity, doing the right thing will be what they think would be the right action rather than acting on something they choose to do instead, or giving in to peer pressure or because someone else is doing it. If they learn to do the best they can, no one can reprimand them for that, because if whatever they did turns out to be wrong, they acted with integrity and showed that they cared and did the best they could with the knowledge they had at the time.

If it feels "wrong", then, it probably is wrong! When you have integrity, you will aim to do the right thing, as you will not want to suffer the guilt afterwards.

Sometimes, doing the right thing may mean that you are the only one to disagree with others, so you don't do the wrong thing. It takes nerve and integrity to be able to say NO under these circumstances.

Teach them to do the right thing because it is right. Teach them to have the courage of their conviction and stand up for themselves, even if the others will laugh at them. If their conscience tells them not to do or to do something, then they must listen. Sometimes doing the right thing means to keep their mouth shut instead of saying something that they may regret later on.

Doing the right thing demonstrates strength of character, especially when it's hard to do the right thing. When someone is genuine and consistent in always doing what's right, it leads to success.

Teach your children to rely on their integrity and honesty and what feels fair and right to them. Doing the right thing means that it can't be to the detriment of anyone else.

> **Sometimes it is better to lose and do the right thing than to win and do the wrong thing.**
>
> *- Tony Blair*

Teach your children as early as possible that there is no win in comparison. All too often children and adult compare themselves with others and often think that others are better than them. This practice cultivates a spirit of low self-esteem.

All this attitude does, is to encourage your children to feel insecure. When you compare yourself to others, you put the emphasis on the wrong person. You can't compare apples with oranges. No matter how alike we think we are to someone else, we are never identical.... (I guess only if you're an identical twin.... even then, they are two individual people with two different minds!) Hence, we can't compare ourselves to anyone else. We have different histories, different issues, different backgrounds and different experiences.

The person to concentrate on, is you, no one else! Teach your children to accept themselves just as they are, warts and all. They are not perfect but neither is anyone else! No one is perfect but they are enough!

Teach your children to embrace the difference and rejoice in others' good fortune. Encourage them to appreciate and celebrate their own little successes as well as those of others.

When your children have an attitude of gratitude, it helps them to avoid comparing themselves with others, as they express gratitude for where they are at in life.

Comparison only leads to unhappiness, insecurity and misery.

Teach your children to focus on what they are about and not on what others are about. This leads to freedom and contentment. If you start this habit early in life and no matter what their friends do, comparison will not be their way, and they will never entertain that negative habit as they grow up.

Comparison only concentrates on what's wrong with them rather than what's right with them. Encourage them to appreciate their talents and the talents of others which may be quite different from theirs, but nevertheless teach them to appreciate that everyone is different and that's wonderful.

We all have our own strengths and weaknesses.

Instead teach your children that if there is an area that they do not excel in to invest in themselves and make every effort they can to improve it. In other words, if they can work on their weaknesses to improve them, they maybe can turn them into a strength. On the other hand, if we try and we can't that's okay, teach them to accept themselves just as they are. Not everyone excels in everything!

Their little friend may be a future Leonardo da Vinci, and if your child's gift isn't to be an artist, that is perfectly fine, but he can rejoice in his friend's talent. Your child may be more gifted for the sciences instead. We all have our own individual gifts and talents. When you have acceptance for yourself and others, there is no need for comparison. There will always be someone with better things than us, someone more intelligent, more beautiful, more athletic, richer etc. So, what? Why do we have to be the same in everything? That's not life! There will always be some who have more than others and that is okay.

Learn to accept what is and teach your children to accept what is.

May be life is unfair sometimes, but no one ever said that it was supposed to be fair! Teach them to give thanks for what they have. If we take what is given to us with a grateful heart, we will attract more positivity in our lives, rather than be envious of what others have got.

In life things can change in the blink of an eye, let's appreciate the present. Everyone goes through trials and tribulations at some point in life. No one escapes! Teach them to appreciate today.

We are all different but unique, but we are all human beings with our own individual paths and journeys to follow. When we compare ourselves to others, we act out of fear and become slaves to fear and allow it to control us which brings unhappiness and insecurity. Let's concentrate on the good, not, the not so good!

Teach your children to allow their weaknesses to become a source of inspiration for them and see where that can lead them. Keep their focus on themselves, not on others. In the future, these "others" may not even be within their radar!

Chapter Eight

How It Works And Parenting Tips

You are your children's best role models.
They are also your harshest critics!

Whatever you do, whatever you say, however you behave, your children are watching! They are also listening! ...... And all of it is being stored and imprinted in their memory to copy one day! So! ..... If you don't want your children to use language that is unbecoming of them or behave in a manner that you do not approve of, don't say it or do it!

The brain as a principle will generalize, edit and distort facts; it will magnify some, cut some out or minimize others. Be aware that your in-house little 'spies' are absorbing everything like a sponge and may not always fully understand what they see or hear with their young minds and may interpret things incorrectly. They will generalize certain principles and adapt them to other things, edit some facts from their experiences and distort the way they remember other memories.

When you are tuned in to your child you can rectify some of these facts.

Your children's little brains are like active recording machines that are constantly taping what they see, hear, feel, smell or taste, as they take information from their environment through their five senses from the time that they are born. These films can be played back at any time in the future.

Childhood memories can continue to be played out throughout life.

If they have recorded wonderful memories, they will be replaying that again and again and feel great each time; however, if their memories are not happy or downright stressful, that is what they will be replaying back over and over in their heads, right through to their adulthood, feeling anxious, depressed and unhappy.

When we recall a memory, we also recall the place, the situation, the people, the colours, the music if any, the weather and the feelings that go with that memory; especially the feelings! Therefore, these feelings, good or bad, can stay with us a lifetime. Sometimes we may not remember the actual memory as such but remember the feelings about something. For instance, we may not remember an incident of being badly scratched by a cat at the age of two, but we remember that we are scared of cats.

By the way you behave with your child and by the way you handle them, and by the experiences you give them, you are given the privilege of giving your children their childhood experiences. Whether they're happy or not depends a lot on the kind of childhood that they experience.

So, if you are in the habit of swearing or throwing or smashing things when things don't go your way, beware! Do not be surprised if your children repeat this same behaviour in the future! .... Good enough for Mummy or Daddy, good enough for me!

And don't say *"I don't know where he gets if from!"*

Remember, it is your children's childhood! If you get it wrong, you can't go back and say: "Let's forget the past few years!"

Your children are only 1 year, 3 years, 5 years, or 7 years etc only once and for a very short period of time. There's no going back to get it right next time. You need to invest in their childhood and get it right first time.

Your children can't relive the same year twice for you to get it right the next time.

Whatever they experience as a child today, will make them the kind of adults that they will be tomorrow. It is important to remember that the way they are treated, the experience of the world that you give them, the values and beliefs that you instil in them will produce the adults that they will be in the future.

You are training your children for them to one day graduate when the time comes and be an independent adult. It is important to make the family and extended family a tension-free zone if it's within your control. Avoid dramas.

You are not just bringing up your sons or daughters, but you are raising maybe a future Prime Minister, a future Nobel Prize winner, a future Researcher, a future Author, a future Scientist, Nurse, Doctor, Accountant, Teacher, Mechanic etc. All of whom, have the power to influence others in society. You have it within your control to give them the childhood that they deserve.

A child who grows up with peace around him will learn to love the world; and the world will love him right back. A child who finds love in the world, will not be looking for antagonism or anarchy.

A child, who experiences tensions in his family of origin, can become an anxious adult who can suffer from anxiety, panic attacks or depression and look for dramas everywhere they go as they misinterpret the world as an adult. They may look for comfort by using drugs and get into the wrong company for acceptance.

Make the atmosphere in the house as relaxed as you can, with plenty of laughter … …. don't forget your sense of humour.......and that doesn't mean letting the kids get away with murder! It is finding the right balance. If they do wrong, it is your job to show them the better way in a constructive manner.

Your children are learning their values in life by what you teach them, by the way you behave, by the way you treat them and treat others and by what they observe.

Many behaviours do not need words for your children to

understand what's going on. And remember, those little eyes don't miss a trick......especially when you think they are not watching!

If respect, dignity, honesty and integrity are important to you, then always behave genuinely in that way, and treat each other and other people with respect, dignity, honesty and integrity at all times. If you show aggression to them and others, they will become aggressive adults.

It is important to be consistent with your beliefs and values so that your children do not receive mixed messages and avoid confusion.

Research shows that boys often follow their fathers and girls often follow their mothers. If as a mother you behave as a victim or a doormat, don't be surprised if your child becomes a doormat as an adult for someone else to wipe their feet on one day!

If as a father your first reaction to everything is aggression, then expect your son to be an aggressive adult one day too. If a child witnesses domestic violence, don't expect them to love and respect their partners one day when they are adults.

Teach your children from an early age that they are not victims and that they are nobody's doormat, but, teach them to be kind and think about others. Teach them to be assertive, rather than aggressive in what they believe and not to allow others to bully them or allow others to put them under pressure to do the wrong thing.

Build their self-esteem and teach them to believe in themselves and to problem-solve.

Teach them to be robust and to be persistent and not to be discouraged and give up if they can't achieve something the first time. Encourage them to keep trying until they are successful. Teach them not to be afraid to venture where they have never ventured before.

Some of these tips may be repeated elsewhere, but it shows how important they are.

Parenting Tips:

1. **Be Reliable**: In other words, don't let your children get away with things sometimes and chastise them for the same things at other times depending on how you're feeling. That means that you have to be unswerving with what you believe in every time. Keep your word.

2. **If you say NO** ...... It's NO! no matter what! Don't just give in after a while and say YES for an easy life.

3. **Think first**, before you say NO – you may end up thinking later that it would have been okay to say YES – and consequently give in.

4. **Parents must discuss and agree** how they will discipline their children and back one another if they don't want the children to play them one against the other – if one parent says NO, and the other parent says YES, the children will soon work you out! If they get the wrong answer from one parent, they will run to the other and try and get the right answer!...... or even I'll ask Grandma! Grandma too must be with the program! You must show unity and support each other. If you disagree with one another, do not do it in front of the children and decide together what you will do.

5. **If you threaten to do something**, you must follow through with what you said – otherwise the children get to know that you won't keep your word and will not take any notice of you. Disciplining them becomes a real battle.

6. **Don't give in** just because they are whining or crying or bribe them to stop. If you do, what you are teaching them is: "If you keep crying or whining, you will eventually get your own way". "The louder you shout you will get what you want." And guess what? ..... prepare yourself for a lot of shouting and screaming .... until they get what they want!

7. **Reward good behaviour.** It doesn't have to be with something expensive. Reward them with praise, cuddles, a star-chart, going to the park or taking them swimming. You can reward

them with hugs and cuddles and let them see how pleased you are with them. It's good to get down to their level, give them good eye contact and tell them why you are pleased with them.

8. ***Ignore bad behaviour as much as possible.*** If they are doing something that's annoying and that irritates you, but they are not doing any harm to anyone or anything............... Ignore them! If you keep paying attention to them at that time, you are fuelling their fire. Pick your battles! Remember, negative attention is still attention. Children would rather have negative attention than be ignored. Be aware not to reward them with cuddles immediately after a negative behaviour. You can give them a cuddle later when they are behaving well, so that they can associate the reward with the good behaviour.

9. ***The rule is simple***: If you want to see a behaviour again, make a fuss of it and praise them; Tell daddy, tell Nana, tell the world! If you do not want to see a negative behaviour again, ignore it or give it very little attention.

10. ***Use Time-Out*** or some other method instead of smacking or yelling at them. If they misbehave while you are out, you can still use time-out. Every room has a corner. Make them face the corner and don't give them any attention. Busy yourself with "filing your nails!"! If a child is two years old, he stays there for three minutes after the behaviour has got better. If a child is three years old, it is four minutes and so on. Main thing is to be consistent! Children soon learn the drill; but they also know if you will eventually give in or if you mean business! Children are psychologically programmed to study and know their parents inside and out!

11. ***Praise***: By praising your children when they behave well, you are building their self-esteem. Having good self-esteem will help them to become well-adjusted adults later and make better choices for themselves. It is helpful to use praise to

change behaviour rather than punishment. It works better than a smack. Make sure you give them good eye contact and tell them why you're praising them. Don't tower above them and ruffle their hair and casually say 'good boy or girl' with no eye contact!

12. ***Inspire your children always.*** Teach them to problem-solve and make the right choices for themselves. Encourage them to try things and not to be afraid of having a go. Help them to take calculated risks. It is better to have tried and failed than never to have tried at all. Encourage them to be free and open.

13. ***Help them to value love and unity in the family.*** Teach them to love each other and to care for one another. Encourage closeness between the siblings. Help them to do things for each other and praise them for it. Always remember they will be looking up to you for approval. They will later treat their husbands, wives, children, in the way that they have been brought up. You are their best role model. So, your job is very important; you are responsible for how the next generation is being brought up!

14. ***Build good memories***: What you do with them today are the memories of tomorrow! Remember, that as children, you, as their parents are helping them build their childhood memories, that they will remember forever as they grow into adulthood and even into their older years. Life is short and we must enjoy the time we have with our children; before long they will no longer be children and as we know tomorrow is not promised to any of us, young or old.

As parents you have been given a great gift: Your children!
They are only children for a small amount of time; they are only lent to you just for a little while.......until they become strong enough to spread their wings in the big wide world!
If you have to tell your children about something that they have done and you need to discipline them, do it with kindness but with

firmness. Doing it that way is to be kind to them and at the same time, they are getting clear messages of right from wrong. Spoiling them and letting them do whatever they want is not being a good parent and kind to your children! So, practice giving them the best experience you can, when they are children, so that they can become fully fledged adults who are able to think of others, who are confident, independent, kind, loving, intelligent, compassionate and passionate about life and make the best choices for their lives.

15. ***Enjoy their childhood***. As their parents you have the joy to be able to write on the slate of their lives, so, make what you write count! But most of all aim for them and for you to enjoy every minute of their childhood, as you too can't go back on these parenting years and enjoy them again.

16. ***Banish negativity***: Far too many people in this world are negative. They see the bad before they can see the good. What we think about we create in our world. Negativity very often starts in childhood because it is modelled to the children by their parents. Help them to see what's right before they can see what's wrong.

17. ***Use constructive criticism***. It is better to try to be accepting and constructive about any criticism, rather than just simply negatively criticize them. When you are constructive, the child learns and feel loved instead of being criticized for the sake of it. That way you are enhancing their self-esteem instead of deflating it.

A child that lives with criticism learns to condemn.
A child who lives with acceptance finds love in the world.

CHAPTER NINE

Some Parenting Challenges

Part 1

The sign of great parenting is not the child's behaviour. The sign of truly great parenting is the parent's behaviour.

- Andy Smithson

Faddy eaters can stress parents out

Many, many children are fussy eaters. If you have a fussy eater don't think that you are the only one who has been afflicted with a fussy child who refuses to eat all the delicious meals that you so carefully prepare for them. A fussy eater, didn't just target you out of the blue to be their parents to stress you and make you suffer!!! It's not personal! The more you talk about food in front of them, the worse they get! The harder you try, the more difficult they seem to get!

It is a very, very common problem with younger children, but there is hope! What matters is how you handle your fussy eater. Being a fussy eater is part of a child's development. It's often their way of exploring their environment as they try to be independent. It can often end up as a battle of the wills, which can be very stressful on both the child and parents' sides.

Children's appetite goes up and down and depending on what's happening in their environment; how active they have been and how much they are growing at the time. If they have a growth spurt, they can easily eat you out of house and home, but when they aren't, they may not be fussed by food at all.

Your child may complain about the look of the food, the colour of it, the texture of it or the shape of it. I have some childhood's memory about eating pumpkin! I believe the dog had more of it than me! However, most children as they grow up, are less likely to keep being fussy eaters. With praise, patience and encouragement, they can become more adventurous. The one mistake that many parents make is that once the child shows a dislike for a certain food, they tend not to offer them that same food again.

As children, they may not like something one day, but enjoy it the next. At that age, they can change with the wind! So, if they don't like something one day, try it again after a few days. If you keep doing that and make food time a happy time, one day your child will be able to enjoy a wide variety of foods and textures, especially if you praise another child for eating their food that your child refuses to eat.

My son used to ask me "Mummy why do you want me to eat trees?" .... when I gave him Broccoli to eat. On reflection, it might have been better to give it to him disguised! If they don't like the look of something, camouflage it in something else, like mash potatoes or a quiche. As children grow up, their tastes buds are forever changing. What they didn't eat yesterday, they may like the next day.

Children eat better when they are eating together with the family or with other children. We must also be realistic about what we expect our children to eat. It has to be age appropriate. Some think that they have a fussy eater, but when they tell you how much the child eats, you discover that the child eats 3 age-appropriate meals a day but is a little fussy over their snacks. Others have a snack may be two hours before dinner time. Consequently, when it comes to dinner time, the child has no appetite. It is better to cut the snacks if it means that they are not going to eat their main meals.

As a child, if their blood sugar drops in the afternoon, and you give them a cup of orange juice, that is enough to raise their blood sugar and for them not to want to eat their dinner. It's best to make dinner a little earlier and if they are still hungry to give them something else afterwards. Be realistic about how much your child should be eating, keeping their age in perspective.

We must not just look at what they are not eating and panic. We must look at the whole child:

- Does your child look healthy?
- Is he well hydrated?
- What's his colour like? Is he pale or has a healthy-look or rosy cheeks?
- Does he have energy to run around and play, learn and explore?
- Or does he just want to lie down and do nothing?
- If you are concerned it is always helpful to visit your doctor or Child Health Nurse; some children can look very pale, especially in the winter, or they may be anaemic and lacking in vitamins. But if your child only eats a small range of foods, it is best to get them checked.

It is important to have good eating habits from the start. Make meal times low-stress, fun, and happy. Your child's willingness to eat will depend on their eating environment. If the child is in a stressful situation, they will not want to eat.

If you are a clean-freak, be prepared for food to drop on the floor and drinks on the table. Never show to your child that it stresses you! You may have to put a plastic on the floor to contain the mess. When they are still small, play aeroplanes etc. to encourage them to eat their dinner! Again, reward good behaviour with lots of praises and ignore bad behaviour as much as possible.

As parents of growing children, you want to fuel their little bodies with as much goodness as you can so that they can grow up strong and healthy. But as you know, as parents of a toddler, pre-schooler or adolescent, the children don't really see it the way you do, do they?

Some toddlers can be a nightmare to feed. Sometimes, when you look back at the day and see what they've actually eaten, it brings you to tears and you think that you are killing your toddlers!!! Relax!

One word of reassurance: No child has ever starved themselves to death! Adults have, but not children!

If they are starving, they will eventually eat!

Though, sadly, some parents have starved their children to death through neglect and being evil! The fact is, if you are worrying whether your child is getting enough nutrients, you definitely are not one of them!!! Although it does happen, it is also extremely rare and you wouldn't be looking for advice to help your child if you were one of those parents!

The secret is in the attitude of the parents towards food and how stressed they are about their children's eating! Some mothers have a knot in their stomachs before they give their children their food... ... and then, wonder why the children don't want to eat it! If as a parent you have had or have an eating disorder, it is best to get professional advice specific for you and your child, so that your child does not pick up on it.

Let me tell you a secret: If you are stressed, your children have special little antennas that can detect it a mile off... ...YES! even though you put on that brave smile and do the pretending act of being calm! They are incredible little human beings with magical powers, whose only job has been to study you from even before they were born! The way it seems to work is that if you are stressed, they can show themselves as little monsters, which stress you twice as much; but if you're having a great day, they are little angels!

Your children react to the moods and feelings that you are in.

Toddlers can turn into little dictators once they turn two! These years can be especially trying. They may have eaten very well from the beginning and suddenly turn into "don't like this!" "don't like that". The problem is, life is too busy! It's too exciting! They have to discover the world and certainly if something has got to go, it will not be their activities!....... "Can't you see I'm too busy? I haven't got time to stop and eat!!! .... That would mean that I have to stop running and sit down! That would mean that I have to stop playing!!!.......NOOO WAY!!!.......and now you want me to use the potty as well?? NOOOO WAY!!!!" ... ...

Don't panic!!! This IS normal! Just part of their development. The more stressed you get about it, the worse it becomes.

Relax! Eventually all will go back to normal!

The problem often is "a power play". They're challenging you......OH! but don't you get angry, ... it's ok!.......Dare I say, it's normal! ....and, YES! it will improve with time!!!! Do not allow them to see that their antics bother you! Use your sense of humour and make it fun.

As the saying goes: you can take a horse to water but you can't make it drink it! Your child has been told from the time he was born what to do, what to wear, when they should sleep, where they should sit etc, but they have worked out now that you can't actually make them eat something ... . in fact, anything if they don't want to! ... . They get to choose whether they eat it or spit it out!!!! Yeah!!! ... . "I can do that! I can do what I want!!!!!....and if you upset me or force me?.......... I can vomit it!!!......and you know what else I've discovered, while we're at it? ... . You can also put me on the potty, but you can't make me use it either!!!! ..... YEAH, I can choose when I want to use the potty as well!!!" ... ... but that's for another time!...... So, as you can see, as parents, you need to be one step ahead!

Some facts about children's eating habits:

It is important to know a few facts about fussy eaters, so that you can understand your own child.

- Appetites are forever changing.
- Children's appetites are affected by their growth patterns. Even as babies, their appetites change. Sometimes they have a long feed and sometimes they have a five-minute feed or else they may go through a full bottle at one time when the next they may only take half of it. Children between 1 and 6 years sometimes can be starving one day, and picky the next. So, rather than worry about their weight weekly, you have a much better idea what their weight is doing if you check it monthly or even two-monthly! It avoids you stressing weekly if you can't see much weight gain.
- Your children's taste buds are different to yours. What you think tastes nice is probably not very nice to them and vice-versa.
- Children get very excited exploring the world about them rather than having to stop to eat. They would much rather play!
- Children are programmed to test the boundaries of what we consider acceptable behaviour. Some can be very strong-willed indeed, especially when it comes to food; whether to eat or not; or what they choose to eat or not to eat. It forms part of their emotional, social and intellectual development.
- The attitude with which we introduce food to our children is crucial. If we are negative and think that they won't like it, then they won't! If we are more positive and make food fun, they are more likely to enjoy their food.
- You may be aware that you would like your children to eat, fish, meat, chicken, eggs, and give them plenty of vegetables and fruits. However, the reality is that your fussy eater will completely disagree with you. If they could survive on fruit juices, some would! .... because, they may have worked out that it is a lot easier to swallow than to chew...especially meat!
- Encourage their independence and allow them to decide how much they want to eat of what they have on their plate. By

providing healthy options for your child at least you know that what they choose to eat will be good for them. If you allow them to choose an option, give them two choices (only!); if they can't decide, you choose. If you give them more than two or three options, it can be very confusing for them. For example: Do you want an orange or a banana? (It's the same for other choices too. For example: Do you want the blue dress or the pink one?)

- If you give your fussy eater any kind of juice before their meal, it may just be enough to raise their blood sugar for them to refuse to eat. So, any drinks in between meals must be plain water if you want them to eat their next meal.

- You need to become very creative, maybe give them a good portion of what they like to eat with a tiny .... or maybe the tiniest portion ...... of what you want them to start eating. If it comes close to their lips, applaud and tell them how marvellous they are and praise them. If you're lucky, the next time, it may actually go in!

- If your child doesn't like his fruits and vegetables, present them in funky shapes and blend the vegetables so that they don't recognize what they are. For example, carrots or broccoli can be mashed with mashed potatoes and if they like cheese, put some cheese on top. Cheese can disguise anything and it gives them calcium! Make them think it's a special treat!

- Do not talk about food in front of them. Yes, it is stressful to you and it may relieve some of your stress by discussing this issue with your mum, partner or with a friend. However, the minute that your fussy eater realises that he is getting a lot of attention by not eating, he will continue to "blackmail" you! Wait, until they are asleep to phone mum or a friend. The only time that you mention food in front of them is to praise them and tell someone else how wonderful they are at eating their dinner, their carrots etc.

- I suggest you don't tell them that if you do not eat your dinner, you can't have any dessert either, which is the way many of us have been brought up. The problem with that thinking is that sometimes, two-year-olds, can eat very, very little throughout the day and can be very, very stubborn; if you've told them that they can't have any desert either, then, you are punishing yourself with massive guilt by sending them to bed with no food at all. However, I do not suggest that you give them chocolate brownies or chocolate fudge cake for desert (I, too would probably leave my meal if I knew that this was for desert!) .... Use yoghurt and fruit for desert. They have to wait for everyone to finish before they can have the fruit and yoghurt. Then, scrape their plates in the bin, in front of them. They may not want their food but are not happy about you throwing it away without saying anything! At least if they have a piece of fruit and a yoghurt before bedtime, you will be able to rest easier too, knowing you haven't completely starved your child.

- Do not make a fuss about them not eating their food or discuss that they are refusing to eat when you're all seating at the table, ignore them as much as possible but praise them if they have eaten any small amount. Be sure to praise their sibling who is eating well. Same principle: reward good behaviour and try and ignore poor behaviour! Keep the conversation at the table light hearted even though you're feeling quite stressed... ... Remind yourself, that your child won't die, just because he is a fussy eater.

- Giving extra vitamins A, C, and D may be useful .... however, stick to the recommended dosage. Not all vitamins are water-soluble. More, doesn't necessarily mean better! If you are really concerned that your child is eating very little, it may be an idea to give them some vitamins, which will help them... ... and you can relax a little! It is always a good idea to check with your doctor first. Monitoring their weight and height monthly, will help you to determine whether they are losing weight or not and growing, staying the same or even gaining weight and growing.

- Sometimes when a child is anaemic, they lose their appetite, so it may be worth seeing your doctor to exclude any health issues. Your child may be given an iron supplement or a tonic to help their appetite.

- If they do not eat their breakfast or lunch do not let them snack on biscuits or chips in between meals. Cut out snacks. Give water only in between meals, and if they are hungry, they have to wait until the next meal…… and they will eat, knowing there's nothing to snack on until the next meal! Maybe, you can be kind and bring the meal a little forward. If they are hungry, they will eventually end up eating it, knowing that you won't give in and offer them chocolate brownies or cookies instead! If they eat, Oh My Goodness! You can praise them to anyone who happens to walk into your life!!!!!

To recap:

- It's difficult to keep saying to be consistent, but with children, they need for you to remain dependable, so that they can feel secure and rely on you and follow your instructions for their good.

- Be clear and concise in how you communicate with them; make sure that they have understood what you meant; be simple; encourage good behaviour; know when enough is enough. Any massive tantrums are best avoided otherwise they won't touch the food.

- Pick your battles. Pick the ones, you know you can win or the ones that you have to win, for their own good!

- Make meal times a social occasion, regular and relaxed and enjoyable, without any phones or electronics in sight.

- Have realistic expectations. If they are really fussy, just ask them to try bringing a small bit to their mouth, congratulate them and make a big fuss of them then gradually a little more on a spoon and gradually increase. It may take you a few days to achieve just that much! Sometimes, if you can get them to take a couple of mouthfuls over time, you may just have to be happy with that... ......just know that this is the child whose appetite you will not be able to satisfy when they are teenagers!!!!! They will always be hungry and constantly asking for food!

- Praise goes a long way! Children and teenagers respond well to praise. If they as much as try a bit of something new, tell Daddy, tell Nanna, tell the world how wonderful they have been! The next time hopefully, they will want to be praised again and will do a little better!

- Never get upset with your child because he's not eating and punish them. This becomes a very stressful situation and they are more likely not to want to eat and you will lose that battle! They will associate food with punishment. They will have lots of other opportunities to try new foods. No point stressing over it.

- As children grow up, their taste buds change. Things they didn't like before, they can now eat happily. No point stressing! If they are fussing over their foods, try and ignore it as much as you can. Give your attention to the child who is eating well and praise them.

- When you give a fussy eater a lot of attention for not eating, you are rewarding their behaviour; they are then, more likely to keep that negative behaviour going. Your children love your attention, even negative attention. Negative attention is better than no attention!

- Reward good behaviour (when they eat) and ignore bad behaviour (when they don't eat) as much as you can (or when they are fussing). Don't let them hijack all your (and the family's) attention during meal times and ignore everyone else. You could try making a star (reward) chart.

- It is a good idea to be able to eat together as a family as soon as you can do it. If, you can't do it for different reasons, that's ok; you may be able to do it when your circumstances change or eat together one day a week. However, eating together, is a good long-lasting habit to teach your children. When they see you and the other members of the family eating, they are more likely to do the same. It is a good time to teach them good table manners too.

- If they have finished before the others and are itching to get off their chair, then teach them the good manners of learning to excuse themselves before they get down. Teach them to ask you, "Please may I leave the table?" and "Thank you for my dinner/Lunch/ Breakfast." Expressing gratitude in the small things leads to expressing gratitude for bigger things.

- If your child is too hyper or distracted before their meal, try having a quiet time before the meal. Take the time to visit the toilet and don't be hasty with the hand-washing ceremony, to give them time to calm down and tell them a short funny positive story. If you don't know one, invent one!

- Try to eliminate other distractions, such as the television, especially if their children's program is on. They can get so engrossed that they would rather be in front of the television instead of eating. Use it as a good opportunity for the family to get together and talk… …… (and of course no electronic game or phone at the table!)

- Encourage your children to help you in the kitchen in the preparation of the family meals as soon as they get old enough. If they think they've cooked the food, they are more likely to eat it. They can help cut fruits or sandwiches in funky shapes or help with salads or prepare vegetables or make cakes or biscuits, depending on their age and dexterity (Safety being paramount). Try and make food fun! Especially the healthy variety! Offer a variety of healthy, nutritious foods and show your children that you are not afraid to try something new. In fact, it is fun and rewarding! Make food look attractive. You can try putting it in interesting shapes and sizes, such as a face. For example: Peas for eyes, a carrot for the nose, a bit of tomato or cucumber for the mouth! Offer them a variety of different colours; they will find it fun and more likely to eat.

- Teach them also to help with clearing the table as soon as they can carry something! If you don't trust them, with your plates, they can clear the place mats or break-proof salt and pepper pots or beakers. As they get older, they can help fill the dishwasher and unload it or wash and dry up the dishes.

- Usually offer your child about 20 minutes to eat. If they have not eaten in those 20 minutes, you then take their plate and scrape it in the bin .... Yes! Even if it upsets them! They can have a yoghurt because it will give them the calcium that they need or a piece of fruit. They have nothing else to eat until the next meal or snack time. Only drink water in between meals, no fruit juices.

- Your children are always observing your reactions! Sometimes they may not even want to try something just so that they can see what you will do and how far they can go to try and assert their will.

- Keep your calm!....... even though you may have an urge to wring their neck... ... DON'T DO IT! .... It's too many years in prison!!!! Just chill, *smile*, and praise someone else who is eating well and try not to notice the fussy one if you can.

- A fussy child may need to see some foods 10 to 15 times before it becomes familiar enough for them to decide to try something new.

- Try offering foods from the 5 recommended good food groups (Dairy, fruit, grain (cereal) foods, lean meats, poultry, fish, eggs, tofu, nuts, and seeds; vegetables, legumes and beans). For example, if your child doesn't like milk but they like cheese, they will be getting their calcium all the same. Relax! If your child refuses something that they used to love, don't fall into their trap! They are trying it on! They're hoping that you will say: "Ok, then, you can have your desert. Would you like your chocolate mousse now?" ... . If you too knew you would get something delicious instead of eating your broccoli, wouldn't you try this little trick too?......(thank God, my son didn't work that one out!) Shame! It's too late!...... YOU are the parent NOW! If they don't want it one time, you can encourage them but ignore it that time, but offer it again to them at another time.

- If you want your child to try something new, make sure that they are hungry and have not filled up on fruit juice or snacks beforehand.

- Encourage your children to share food with other children. They often eat better when other children are eating with them at the table. They're more likely to try something new if their friend is enjoying it. So, from time to time invite some of their little friends to lunch or dinner.

Do Bribing And Punishing Work?

It isn't a good idea to use punishment where food is concerned.

It would immediately link food with something negative; if they don't feel like eating, they would be less likely to eat. Some can be very stubborn. You will not win this battle by punishing them, but you may if you keep calm and refuse to stress over their food.

It is also very tempting to offer bribes (treats), as the child may eat that one time, but would expect the bribe every time too! The only problem is that your child would more than likely be more interested in the treats than in the healthy food! It also gives the child the idea that healthy eating is something negative and the treats are the only positive.

So, if you have a fussy eater, the message to you parents is:

Don't despair! Children are forever going from one phase to another! Just when you think that you've got one phase sorted out and feel on top of it, they then go onto another phase! Relax! Some are very fussy eaters between 2 years and 4 years old, but by the time they turn 5 and go to school they will want to eat you out of house and home! And when they become teenagers, you will never be able to fill them up!

Chapter Ten

Some Parenting Challenges

Part 2

Childhood Obesity

> *Obesity in children is growing out of control. A big part of this is economic. Fake foods are more affordable. It's enticing people to eat more because they think they're saving money when they're really just buying heart disease.*
>
> *- Jillian Michaels*

If you think you have problems when you have a fussy eater, just try having children who want to keep eating and as a consequence keep piling on the weight! Children are strange little beings sometimes! Some are reluctant to eat whilst others can't get enough of it!

Unfortunately, many parents can make a false neuro-association between food and love… …. "I love you, so I feed you!". They see food as a way of showing their child how much they love them.

It's the same kind of thing that when the children have flown the nest to go to University, College or moved away from home. When they come back home for a visit the mother prepares to cook their favourite foods for each of the days that their grown-up children will grace them with their presence.......Including doing their washing etc.... (but that's another story!).

There is this big connection between showing love and wanting to treat your children with the lovely foods that they enjoy.

The Food of Love

Many parents often equate love with food. So, whatever the children want they can have, whether it is good for the child or not, because they love them. Some young children can become obese because their parents are constantly giving them special food treats as a symbol of their love, not realising that they are harming their children in the process.

Food has nothing to do with how much you love your children. Every other parent loves their child just as much as you do!

The problem is, if that attitude starts early in their childhood, where the mother or father equates food with love, then they also rationalize it by thinking if I refuse them the treats and foods that they love, that they are not showing their children a lot of love.

The danger which goes with that trend of thought is.... If the child refuses their food, then, it is also possible for those mothers or fathers to confuse things and see it as a rejection of their love, causing many psychological problems on both sides. That kind of thinking brings a lot of difficulties. It is not rational thinking and bad habits for the child to take as they grow up into teenagers and later on as adults.

The food that you feed your children with has nothing to do with the love that you have for them or how your children feel about you! Another issue that can happen if the parents go along this line of thinking, is that there's enormous guilt about refusing to give their children constant treats. The children will ask for the treats because they like the taste and know how their parents will react; if you are used to caving in after a little while, the children will nag and pester until they get what they want. They will do what they're best at!

However, you as a parent, do not have to grant your child's wishes if it's not the right thing for them, just so that you can feel better.

As a parent, your job is clear: you do what's right for your child not what your child demands.

However, there is the danger, that if you keep feeding your child with everything that they fancy, whether it's good for them or not, is that gradually, as they get older, the weight accumulates and results in your child becoming overweight, which is only a step away from obesity!

If a child requests milk or worse still juice in a bottle most of the day as it is their comfort, you may feel bad saying no to them, as you know that you are taking their comfort away from them. This is the scenario, when you see a five-year-old with rotten carried teeth when they start school. If they have had juice in a bottle for the last 3 years, then you may as well have rinsed their mouth with sugar all day, for the last 3 years. Even if they had milk bottles all day, they may have problems with the enamel of their teeth by then!

The incidence of obesity has increased dramatically in the past decades in Australia as well as in the United Kingdom, America and many other western countries as those countries continue to prosper.

Obesity is a major health problem and among the principal risk factors to ill-health in Australia. This factor also has negative consequences on our economy, especially when considering the medical costs due to the sequalae following obesity throughout life.

As much as some parents feel that they have difficulties with children who are fussy eaters, other parents have the opposite problem. Because of the association of love and food, to some giving their children food is to be nice to them. There are some children and adolescents who can keep eating and eating, for the sake of it, because it tastes good or for comfort; especially if they have seen you, as their role model do the same; if something goes wrong and you feel stressed, you reach out for the biscuit tin or the chocolate bars! ... ... but you don't just take one, you just eat the lot until you feel that you have filled your emotional hole! Your children are little copycats who will copy you! They will duplicate what you do and will see nothing wrong with it! The more they eat the larger their stomachs get; the larger their stomach gets the more they need to eat for them to feel satisfied.

The Web Report (last updated 24th November 2017) notes that at age 18 to 21, 15% of those born from 1994-1997 were obese compared with 8% of those born in 1974-1977. Adults in 2014-2015 were more likely to be obese than those of the same age 20 years earlier at all but 1 age. Nearly two-thirds (63%) of adults were overweight or obese in 2014-2015; the proportion who are obese increased over time.

One quarter (26%) of children and adolescents were overweight or obese in 2014-2015. That's around 1.2 million of children and adolescents. (Web Report)

The Origin of Adult Obesity

Our food habits and traditions stem from our childhood and how and what we were allowed or encouraged to eat. Often obesity run in families because of the food that they eat. Your children will do what you do.

The majority of adults who are now obese or overweight has its origins in childhood.

Therefore, obesity is as much a childhood problem as it is an adult one. School uniforms have had to be made sizes bigger and more generous for today's children.

This is very concerning as those habits that we adopt as children continue with us the rest of our lives, causing many health problems such as Diabetes type 2, high blood pressure, strokes, and cardiovascular problems. The other problem is that we reproduce the same difficulties in the next generation and give them an earlier opportunity to suffer these health issues even earlier.

How We Talk About Food Matter

What we say to our children about food matters. If we tell them that they can't leave the table until everything on their plate has been eaten then we encourage them as they grow older to eat everything that's put in front of them no matter whether they are hungry or not, no matter if it is healthy or not. It becomes automatic, if it's in front of them, they'll finish it, with not a thought whether they're still hungry or even want it or not! How many of us are guilty of doing this? ... ... I, for one has to confess that I was (or sometimes still is) one of them! We pile on so many extra calories which eventually accumulate and turn into fat, just because we were brought up this way; not because we are hungry, not because we like it even, but just because that's what has been expected of us since we were a child and it's now a habit!

Food is to nourish us with not to comfort us with or to eat it out of habit. We need to eat "consciously"; in other words, we need to eat but as soon we feel that we've had enough, we must stop!

We become very accustomed to serve larger and larger portions; when we go to a restaurant and ask for a dish, there usually is enough for two people on the one plate, if we are unlucky! .... often, there's enough for three! And the funny thing is, that we see it as normal! If we get served less, then we complain that they were mean with their portions!!! Consequently, adults and children keep on piling on the weight resulting in the obesity problem which now affects everyone.

Appetites vary at different times; some days, we eat more than others and sometimes we don't really have an appetite. Children especially eat more when they are having a growth spurt than when they're not. If they are expected to finish everything on their plate and it becomes their life's motto, because this is what they have always done, then you are encouraging your children to become obese adults.

Some parents don't like to waste food, (a leftover habit passed down from the wars, I think!) they either finish their children's plates or else they force the children to finish it themselves. That is not a good practice to adopt either. Those love handles get bigger and bigger and you and your children put on unnecessary weight, putting them at risk of being ridiculed and bullied by their peers.

These are childhood habits that have repercussions in adult life, with poor health consequences. Your children won't die if they are not very hungry sometimes. It's part of life that appetites vary according to what the child does or whether they are having a growth spurt or not.

Drinks

Sometimes, children may think that they are hungry, when in fact they are dehydrated and need to drink water instead. Keep them well hydrated – with water. Avoid giving your children fizzy drinks. Many of these fizzy drinks contain high sugar levels, which interfere with your children's blood sugar levels and encourage them to gain weight and develop early type 2 Diabetes. When you give them a drink, stick to water. There is nothing better!

Some tips to avoid obesity:

- Teach your children to drink plenty of water to keep well hydrated.
- Teach your children to eat until they are full. If there is still food left on the plate after they are full, they do not need to finish it. They can leave it without getting into trouble.
- Teach them that they do not need to continue eating just because it tastes good. They can stop when they feel full, even when it tastes "yummy". It's a good habit to adopt as a child instead of fighting the bulge all their lives as an adult.
- Teach them to have the usual three structured meals a day: Breakfast, lunch and dinner. If they are hungry before their meal, they can have an apple or wait until lunch or dinner, instead of having sugary snacks in between meals. Perhaps their meal times can be brought up a little earlier when this

happens. Give them plenty of fresh fruits and fresh vegetables. If you give snacks, make them healthy snacks such as fruits or a piece of cheese.

- Teach them not to use food to fill up their emotional issues. Food is to nourish them not to comfort them when they are feeling down. Encourage them to talk when they feel they have emotional issues to be resolved.
- Teach them that if they have a biscuit or snack as a treat, that they only have one, not the whole packet, just because they like it.
- Teach them portion control. Be aware of not giving them large plates so that you get tempted to fill them. Every plate has an inner circle. Fill the inner circle not the whole plate!
- Encourage them to enjoy the fresh air and to participate in physical activities when they are still small. Exercise helps in avoiding obesity as they burn calories. Exercise forms part of the essential for a healthy childhood.

Overweight Children are an Easy Target for Bullies

Obesity puts your children at risk of being bullied in school or clubs that they attend, including giving them real health issues, all caused by over-eating and lack of exercise.

It becomes a vicious cycle: because they are overweight, they find it harder to do physical activities and exercises; and because they feel depressed that they can't do what others their age can, they fill their emotional hole by eating more. When they eat more, they get even bigger and therefore are completely demotivated to go out in the fresh air to do any exercises.

This scenario is exciting to a nasty bully who finds pleasure in doing harm to someone who is different from the others. Bullying emotional scars can last them for a very long time, even in adulthood and sometimes these scars never heal.

Some children can be quite cruel and pick on other children who are unlike others; if they notice that your child is a bit on the heavy side they will see them as a good target to tease them and bully them and often be physically and emotionally abusive towards them, and let's not forget cyber bullying through social media for the older children!

This kind of abuse can be very distressing and last a long time before any adult becomes aware of it and can do something about it, if at all. Often the victims themselves are more reluctant to say anything or let anyone know about their demise for fear of further retributions. Those emotional scars that these abusive experiences caused to children can damage and traumatise them, affecting their self-esteem and self-worth. Many end up in therapy as adults long after the actual abuse has ceased. Many teenagers have taken their own lives due to abuse and bullying.

So, if you really love your children, do not overfeed them and keep their weight within the normal Body Mass Index (BMI) range for their age group. (A visit to your nurse or GP will let you know about their BMI).

Obesity is something that can be easily avoided in children because it is you as parents who provide them with the food that they eat, when they are still under your roof. It is rare that obesity is due to some physical problem, like Prader Willi syndrome or such like.

Weight and lack of Agility

The larger we are, the harder it is to displace ourselves. The less exercise we take, the more uncomfortable, the more pain and the more puffed out we are when we do exert ourselves for a little while, which then stops us from doing anymore. The less exercise we do, the more calories we ingest to console ourselves with, the more weight we accumulate! Although it is when we are overweight that we need to exercise more, the children are often not encouraged. The heavier they are, the more awkward they become, and find any physical activity a struggle. At the same time, they fear their peers making fun of them and using it as another reason to bully them and ridicule them, causing poor self-esteem and self-worth.

As Parents Your Weight Matters

It is difficult when both parents or even if one parent is obese, for them to value putting their children on a healthy eating plan to keep their weight within the healthy range for their age. What tends to happen is that the children get used to the family diet; and if the family diet comprises of burgers and chips, or some other fast foods washed down with some fizzy drinks, four to five times a week, with very little fruits and vegetables if at all, the children too will gain weight and become unhealthy.

Often it may be due to ignorance of what constitutes a healthy diet. Having some fast foods once in a while is acceptable, but not as a staple diet. When parents are overweight, it is not comfortable for them to encourage their children to take exercise, as they are quickly puffed out and tired themselves, and to be fair, it feels a bit hypocritical!

The more weight that you carry, the more difficult it is for you to keep up with your children. It is difficult to join them at floor level as getting up or going down becomes challenging on the joints. It is difficult to go to the park to kick a football, as you may have problems with your knees or hips. Consequently, the children miss out on exercise and the weight keeps piling on and they are on their way to future health problems due to obesity.

Some children can create mayhem, if you do not give them the food that they are asking for. If you are a parent that believes in giving in to anything for an easy life, you are harming your child's health. You have to learn to say NO and offer a healthier option. It is never good practice to give in for an easy life. What you thought would be an easy life, becomes fraught with problems and in fact makes life very difficult.

Have you noticed that near almost every school or college, that there are fast foods chain restaurants? Around lunch time, the place is packed with the local students and often around 5pm, there's an enormous queue in the drive-in waiting to be served? Although these days they are more aware of the healthier options most kids do not go to these places to have a salad! Let this be a treat once in a while, rather than something that they have regularly.

Blame

This isn't about blaming but about raising awareness of how dangerous obesity can be to your children and their future and to yourselves. Remember that as parents you are your children's role models. Whatever is good for the goose is also good for the gander!

Your children will do more of what they see you do than what you tell them to do.

If you have unhealthy habits in your lifestyle, then your children will copy you. For a start they won't know that they are being unhealthy, because as far as they are concerned, this is the norm for them! This doesn't only apply to food, but to other things too. If you smoke, there is a high chance that your child will smoke too, especially if you are the same sex parent. If you drink alcohol in excess, there is a high chance of your child copying you too. If you take drugs, they will see nothing wrong with taking drugs as they will be used to it.

Dangers of obese children

Childhood obesity can be very harmful to children in a variety of ways. Obese children are more likely to have:

- High Blood Pressure.
- High cholesterol levels; both of these are high factors for cardiovascular disease.
- Impaired glucose tolerance, insulin-resistance and type 2 Diabetes Mellitus.
- Breathing difficulties.

- Many suffer with sleep apnoea and asthma, which affect their breathing due to their weight.
- Sleep apnoea has many side effects such as the onset of Alzheimer's Disease and Dementia.
- Joint problems and musculo-skeletal problems causing difficulties in moving and more handicapping in adulthood.
- Gastro-oesophageal or gall bladder disorders, and reflux.
- Skin rashes and irritations.
- Discrimination, teasing and bullying by their peers causing poor self-esteem and social isolation, which can carry on, way into adulthood or have a disastrous ending.
- Obese children often become obese adults, which carry risks of cardiovascular disease, high blood pressure, stokes, diabetes, cancers, and fatty liver diseases.
- Obesity in children become more serious when they are adults.

Unfortunately, obesity in childhood is bad news on all levels and it is all avoidable and preventable by educating the parents.

- We need to teach parents about giving their children a healthy childhood, so that the children of tomorrow can have a healthier upbringing, which then leads them to a healthier adulthood. Therefore, it is less of a burden on society, family, better financially, less of a drain on hospitals, medical resources, nursing staffs and doctors.

Tips on avoiding obesity in childhood:

- Sometimes tiny steps can lead to huge achievements. Educating parents about healthy eating and healthy habits can encourage children to have healthier eating habits that they will carry into adulthood and in turn help their children.

- Use the ingredients that your children enjoy to make healthier recipes. If they like fried eggs, try using the eggs to make a quiche and disguise spinach into it.
- Whatever turns them on, make it healthier!
- Avoid making calories-rich dishes; no matter how "yummy" it is!
- Encourage exercise; join them in a bike ride if you are able to. Explain to them the benefits of exercise in their life. Do some physical activity daily with them. Help them to stay active and praise their physical efforts for exercise, no matter how small. Encourage them to come with you on walks, especially if you live somewhere picturesque.
- Reduce the time they stay indoors playing indoor games, especially on computers, iPad, games consoles etc, which only encourages them to be sedentary. Avoid anything that will encourage them to be inactive. You can try putting an obstacle course in the garden for you all to compete with and enjoy. Time them and help them get excited about beating their own time. No matter how long it takes them, reward them on any little success to inspire them.
- Make sure that they have adequate sleep. If they haven't had enough sleep, they will wake up tired and will be reluctant to do any physical activity. Make sure that computers, phones, tablets, iPads, or gaming console are well switched off two or three hours before their bedtime. The same hormones that we have for satiety, are the hormones that help us keep the weight on when we don't sleep well at night time.
- You are your children's best example to adopt a healthy lifestyle and have healthy eating habits and keep active. Give them plenty of fresh fruits and vegetables and whole-grain products. If they are older than 5 years old you can use low-fat dairy products, but not before. Use mono-unsaturated

oil if using oil rather than polysaturated fats and find out the difference between them. In other words, use good fats like Olive oil, Sunflower oil or Avocado oils. Educating yourself on a healthy diet is essential. Choosing lean meats, poultry, fish, lentils and beans are useful. Avoid fizzy drinks, and low-sugar drinks but encourage plenty of water.

- Don't buy chocolate, cakes and keep tempting deserts or puddings in the fridge or pantry at all times. Avoid high-fat and high-sodium foods. Use a fruit like an apple or pear as desert. Once in a while, as a treat, children can be given something that's really tasty but not necessarily in the healthier range. Encourage your child when they keep to their healthy diet and praise them, especially when they are active.

- Make sure that you join a club or have your own support system to help you or join in with some of your friends and support each other.

- Help your children to raise their own self-esteem as every little success that they manage will increase their self-esteem. As parents encourage them, be positive and don't forget to praise every little effort that they make.

- Children should only be put on a weight-reduction diet under the care of a health care professional. Aim at reducing the rate of weight gain, while allowing for normal growth and development.

- Do not let food become a big issue in the household, as th ere is the danger that it may lead to eating disorders later on. Just adopt a healthier lifestyle, without the children thinking that they are being picked on. If they adopt healthy habits, the weight will drop off.

- Good Luck.

Chapter Eleven

Some Parenting Challenges

Part 3

Tell me and I forget. Teach me and I remember.
Involve me and I learn.

- Benjamin Franklin

Stressful Children's behaviours

Tantrums

All parents dread their children's tantrums, especially if they are in public! Definitely when you have an "Oscar-winning performer"! you almost want to join them and let's all have a melt down together!!! It's in the middle of the supermarket? .... who cares???

When it gets that difficult, you need to have thought about it first and have a strategy to cope and maintain your countenance!... as lovely as it would feel to just scream yourself, deep down, you know it's not the thing to do....and my goodness how many eyes will be popping out of their sockets, ready... ... not to blame the child, who is misbehaving... ... but YOU! who just happened to be minding your own business and doing your shopping as any good mother would, when little Johnny started to throw a fit because he couldn't have his way!

Tantrums are extremely common in toddlers and pre-schoolers. As young children, they haven't yet learnt the social skills to deal with difficult feelings, and do not know how to deal with some strong and disturbing feelings; so, they cope with it the best way they know how, which is to shout, scream, yell and lash out and throw themselves on the ground.

If you learn to tune in to your children's emotions, you can pre-empt their tantrums and learn to avoid them all together.

No two tantrums are the same, just as no two children are the same. They are all individuals. Tantrums can take the form of spectacular explosions of feelings, such as anger, frustration and huge screaming fits and lashing out at whoever happens to be in the way, and at times, the child 'loses' it completely.

For others, it may be a little more tamed, but not much more; where you can observe, screaming, tears, sobbing, stiff limbs, throwing themselves on the floor, arching their backs, kicking, or running away. Some can even hold their breath and make themselves turn blue (which has a very panicky effect on the parents – don't worry, they will be okay after their tantrum); others can vomit and become aggressive as part of their spectacular display! Not a pretty picture is it? Have I scared you? Well, you can see why most parents dread these scenes!

On the other hand, there are some children who have very mild tantrums and others who manage to avoid them altogether ... . Must admit, it's pretty rare! Hopefully, the latter will be your child!

Tantrums are very common between 1year and 3 years, as at those ages, they do not have enough social and emotional skills to deal with how they are feeling and how to control themselves, which is known as self-regulation. Sometimes they are overtaken by huge emotions and do not know what's happening to them. It's difficult enough for them to control their body let alone their emotions and feelings. Sometimes, it takes a little more maturity.

At around 2 years of age, at any time when they cannot get what they want, a 2-year-old can throw a tantrum that they can be proud of and keep it going for quite a while. That is the normal way that toddlers deal with difficult feelings before they learn to self-regulate. The more attention you give to their tantrum and behaviour, the longer it lasts. Distracting them or ignoring the behaviour and acting normally around them, can dissipate it quicker.

Why do children have tantrums?

Toddlers social and emotional skills are only just beginning to develop at that age. It's hard to say how you feel when you do not have the words to describe how you feel. Their language skills are still at an immature stage, which means that they often do not have the language to identify what they are feeling and what's going on in their bodies and cannot explain the emotions going through them. It would be like us, going to a foreign country and trying to express to someone how we feel when we don't have the words in their language to say how we are feeling. It's also at the age when they are wanting to be independent but may have separation anxiety. However, they know that if they go out of control that you will have to take notice of them. So, to throw a tantrum is a way to manage their emotions but it also means that they are starting to understand they are not happy with something that's going on around them and want something to change.

You may be surprised that older children too can have tantrums. Some may be socially immature and others may just have not learnt a better way of expressing themselves and managing how they feel. Some may have unwittingly been rewarded for their tantrums by their parents or carers giving in each time they happened to have a tantrum. Consequently, for them, having a tantrum just means that they are going to get their way, no matter how unsociable their behaviour is and how long it lasts because in the end they will get what they want.

All children develop at their own pace. Some may still have

tantrums at a later stage, because, they are evolving emotionally slower than others to develop self-regulation.

Self-regulation is the ability to understand and manage our reactions, behaviour and feelings.

On average it develops around 12 months. As the child gets older and develops, they are much more able to regulate their reactions and are much better able to calm themselves down, when they get upset. Tantrums after that become fewer and fewer. However, before that, around the age of two, the child goes through an egoistic phase or what's commonly known as: "The terrible two's". Tantrums are often more frequent then. But, relax! ......it will pass! Like a lot of other things, it's only a phase that children go through.

There are often different triggers to children's tantrums:

- Often it depends on the child's temperament. Some children are very forceful or "strong-willed". Their temperament is a major factor of how strongly or how often they react to difficult emotions such as frustration or anger. A child who is easily upset about anything is more likely to be prone to tantrums, (It can be that he or she takes after the cantankerous grandfather or uncle!), rather than the child who has a naturally sunny disposition (who may clearly take after the lovely grandma or auntie!...... just joking!)
- When children are tired, hungry, overstimulated or stressed they are more prone to fall victim to tantrums as they are unable to manage their feelings.
- At around the age of two, everything to a child is "Mine"; so, if they have other children playing with their toys, this can be a trigger to a huge tantrum and can cause them to create a volcano of emotions for the parent to deal with. At the same time, you are trying to socialise them and teach them to share. It can be a difficult situation. Other similar

situations that can cause them stress can easily be the cause of other outbursts.

- Any strong emotions that they can't identify or explain such as anger, embarrassment or worry, for example, fear that their mother is leaving (and to some of them it may mean that she may not come back, if mum is not used to leaving them with anyone; to a child it sends panic through them). All of these can be the cause of toddlers' tantrums. They need a lot of reassurance.

Tune in to your child

It is helpful if as a parent you can tune in to your child's feelings and emotions, then you can distract them and actually avoid world war 3 or a massive tantrum. Toddlers can easily be distracted if you get their attention on something else, especially something that they are interested in......may be a T-Rex?

What can you do about tantrums?

- As stress, hunger and overstimulation are key triggers to tantrums, you can try and pre-empt stressful situations. If they are tired, hungry or overstimulated from their playgroups, and you take them to a supermarket, you are looking for trouble. You only do this in cases where the whole family will starve to death if you do not go to the supermarket then. If you can avoid it, you should! Life will be a lot less stressful!
- Know your child! Be aware when they are feeling big emotions, and that it's all about to explode. You can try talking about their feelings but if they have past the point of no return, they will not hear you! Try and distract them instead and you can try talking about their feelings later when they are calmer. Their level of understanding will depend on their maturity.
- Don't give them long explanations that their little brains can't cope with. They will ignore you and scream louder!

- If you know what triggers their tantrums, plan ahead and try and avoid the triggers. If you want to go to the supermarket, make sure that you're not taking a tired, hungry or over-stimulated child with you.
- Gently, try to make them identify what they are feeling and what caused it. For example, "Were you angry because Tom took your Lego?" Then talk about what they could have done instead and encourage them to share. Sharing is part of their socialisation.

For some, no matter how much you try to avoid tantrums, they can throw the biggest tantrums no matter what! This can be so stressful and make you feel quite inadequate in coping with your child's behaviour. But, relax! .... know that the tantrums will stop at some point. You won't still be in the same place in 24 hours! The more stressed you are, the more your child will react to how you are feeling! The calmer you are, the better your child will be.

> *Remember anxiety is contagious, so is calm.*
>
> *- Debbie Pincus*

Some more thoughts on how to cope with tantrums:

- You may be really stressed, but whatever you do, you need to keep calm. Breathe......Remember, you're the grown-up and you're in charge! Yes, it can be really difficult at times, but remember, if you stay calm, you can win; if you don't, it's drama time! The problem is that sometimes, your child can trigger anger in you, but you cannot give yourself the luxury of getting angry. Keep focused on calming the situation down.
- So, Breathe! Breathe! If you concentrate on your breathing it will keep you calm. Your child will react to how you handle the situation. Better still, it you can get your toddler to practice their breathing with you and make it a game. It will

calm them down too. If you teach them breathing exercises and make it fun when they are not having a tantrum, they are more likely to be willing to do it when they are having one. Either way, if they do it, they will calm down. It's worth a try and may work for you. Don't forget your sense of humour too!

- Try and reduce the stress around them as much as possible. If they are tired, hungry or very excitable, they are more likely to fall victims to tantrums. So, if you are going anywhere, make sure that they had a rest, their tummy is full and that you have kept them fairly quiet.

- Keep in tune with your children. If you know them well, you will have an idea when they are more likely to express big feelings and emotions that they are not yet able to control.

- Distraction is a great skill to have with toddlers prone to tantrums. Looking for an imaginary pussy cat or doggy can be a life-saver or talking about the Wiggles or Peppa Pig. However sometimes it doesn't matter how in tune you are with your child if they are going to have a tantrum, they will! That's when you need to know what to do but most of all stay calm.

- If the child is a little older, you may be able to talk about their emotions to them, by naming and acknowledging them. For example, "You were really upset earlier when you couldn't get what you wanted weren't you?" ..... "You cried because you were scared that Mummy wasn't coming back?" You can use that same conversation to reassure them that their parents are always there for them, that they have to go out sometimes but they will always come back. They will be better able to name their emotions later on to you and express themselves and their feelings better, on other occasions and it will make your job easier to deal with them. By acknowledging your child's difficult feelings, you can stop a tantrum escalading to gigantic proportions.

- Once they are in the full swing of a tantrum, it's too late to discuss anything with them. They will not hear you. They are too focused on what they want. Wait it out! But stay close. You going away, will make things worse, so don't feed that monster! Starve it of oxygen by not giving it attention. They will not hear you and frankly, they don't care about what you are saying as they will not see reason.

- Stay in charge. Remember that you're the parent and don't allow them to drag you down by giving in to their whims for peace sake or getting angry and frustrated ...... although it may be very tempting......but if you do that, you would be rewarding bad behaviour. Just because they want something, doesn't mean that they should get it. Use your judgement.

- Ignore anyone else! Have confidence in your ability as a parent. Keep yourself calm and the goal is to get your child to calm down.

- Be consistent! ...... again, that word! But it's the basis for all parenting advice. When you are inconsistent, your child will not know where they are and what's allowed and what's not and they will feel insecure.

- Do not give any attention to whining. If you do, it only gets worse. Ask your child to use their words and to ask properly for what they want.

- Do not accept that they hit you. You can use Time-Out if they hit or bite. You have to check your own behaviour: if you hit them, you cannot tell them that hitting is wrong!

- Be clear and concise in your communication with them.

- Use praise appropriately. Children appreciate being praised and encouraged. If they've had one of those days, when everything they've done has been naughty, you have to catch them maybe just sitting down for a moment, to tell them what a good boy or girl that they are sitting down nicely! Or else ask them to do something small for you so that you can praise them, like offering a biscuit to their brother or sister, so that you can tell them how marvellous they are for thinking of their sibling! If you see good behaviour, be over-the-top enthusiastic about it and always praise good behaviour.

- Even at that age you can teach them as early as they can understand that their actions have consequences. You can also use these consequences to try and prevent further bad behaviour.

- Give tantrums as little attention as possible. Be aware not to reward tantrums by giving in to what you had told them they couldn't have or by giving lots of hugs during a tantrum. Give them the attention when they are good afterwards not when they are misbehaving. To children any attention is better than no attention. Even if you keep talking to them, telling them off, shouting or pleading or bargaining with them, it is still attention... ...... it is far better than being ignored! You are just fuelling the fire! Remember, negative attention is still attention! So, starve the tantrum of attention by talking as little as is necessary at the time.

- Try and make sure that you feel supported during those difficult times, as children's tantrums can cause a lot of stress to the parent looking after the child. If your child is having a tantrum don't react straight away. Sometimes it happens as the child likes to see your reaction. If you give them a lot of attention, they can keep going for a long time. If you take a little time to go to the bathroom (providing it's safe) and wash your hands, things may have calmed down by themselves; by then their attention may have gone onto one of their toys.

- Decide on what plan you will use to cope with a tantrum before it happens. Be clear in your head and execute your plan when the situation arises. Know what you will do before it gets to the point where you find yourself in the middle of a full-blown tantrum and have no idea what to do.

- If you're a control-freak, a tantrum will freak you out because you can't control your child's emotions and feelings.

Therefore, learn that your child's emotions belong to them and it's not something that you can control. You can try reducing the triggers but sometimes no matter what and how you have pre-empted their tantrums they can still go into one! Accept what is! Accept that tantrums are a normal part of their development and that it takes time to learn self-regulation skills; and that as they grow, the tantrums will diminish and that there's no need to get stressed out over them... .... Dare I say, that one day you will laugh about it???...... Your aim at that time is to keep yourself calm and keep your child safe and out of harm's way, and when they are calmer you can help by controlling their behaviour to try and prevent further episodes.

- Sometimes, some parents can think that the child is deliberately throwing a tantrum to make them pay for something or to spite them. That is not true! Don't go there! Don't put an adult head on young shoulders. An adult brain may reason this way but a child reacts spontaneously to what's happening in the moment. They do not have this adult way of thinking... ...you did this to me, now I'm getting my own back! Children do not think in such a complex way. Things are a lot simpler for a child. So, don't fall in that trap! Don't go with that train of thoughts. It only makes the situation much worse. Your child will pick up on your feelings and things will get worse. Your child just doesn't have the skills right now to cope with how they are feeling and what's happening around them.

- If you think that you've had enough and finding it difficult to cope and that you may harm your child, it is much better to put distance between you, by putting the child in their bedroom where they can't harm themselves. Go and calm down and have a cup of tea or phone a friend who you know can help you and calm you down.

- Don't worry about other people judging you. Concentrate on what your plan is to cope with your child's tantrum. There will always be people who will feel for you and there will also be people who are quick to judge you. If they judge you, they don't even deserve a second thought. They've either forgotten what it was like for them or don't have children and are very judgemental; therefore, their opinion doesn't matter! Don't let them worry you. Most of all, you must not judge yourself as a bad parent because your little Johnny has more tantrums than his little friend who is an angel! Our children are born with their own individual personalities with their own temperaments, gifts and talents and they develop at their own rate. I don't think that this is backed up by research but I believe that those children are usually very bright!
- And lastly, remember that you have a sense of humour. Find the funny side of things so you can have a good laugh about it later. Whatever you do, do not let your child see you laugh or think that you are laughing at them. Even though they are still quite small some can really feel quite offended and you would have made things worse.

As parents, you are only human and yes, you will make mistakes; but at the time you are doing the best you can with the knowledge that you have at that particular time. No one can ask you for more than your best. All you can do is every time you make a mistake is to acknowledge it and learn from your mistakes... ... By the time they are all grown up, you would have got it all sorted out!

.... And when you will want to give advice to your adult children, they will tell you "but Mum, you're out of date! We don't do it like this anymore!"

Oh, well, that's life!

Chapter Twelve

Some Parenting Challenges

Part 4

There is no such thing as a perfect parent. So just be a real one.

- Sue Atkins

Teenage Tantrums And Behaviours

Just as toddlers can have tantrums that can be quite distressing to their parents and to themselves, teenagers and adolescents' poor behaviour can cause a lot of heartache to their parents and family too and to themselves.

Strangely enough, the cause of teenage tantrums is not dissimilar to those of the toddlers as these teens have grown up without learning proper self-regulation. Their behaviour is due to emotional immaturity. They find themselves unable to control their strong feelings and emotions. They have no better social skills than to fight, scream and shout to get their own way. It is scarier because you are dealing with a teenager who can physically be quite tall, strong and powerful but behaving in a very immature way.

Many have poor self-worth, self-control and self-esteem and

haven't learnt any social techniques to self-regulate, not even to breathe and calm down first, so that they do not emotionally hijack themselves. Often, there can be a lot of heartache on both the parents and teenagers' sides, because the teenagers have misunderstood certain things and do not have the maturity needed to deal with it as they should.

What the teens need when they are in distress is to feel that they have been listened to; that it is safe for them to say how they feel. A lot of the time they shout because they feel that nobody is listening to them and no one has heard what they are saying. They need to feel better about themselves.

They need help to raise their self-worth and self-esteem, instead of coming down on them hard and making them feel even more worthless. This may be easier said than done of course! The words that you use are very important. Try not to use words that are excitable like, furious, hate, devastating, nasty, selfish or evil. It's vital that you do not belittle them and keep your calm. Try using words like: calm, breathe; I'm trying to understand; I hear you; when you can calm down we can talk about it better; I want to hear what you have to say; Let me help you. Don't shout over them. Remain calm even though it may be very hard. If the tantrums happen on a regular basis, it may be useful to get a referral for some Cognitive Behaviour Therapy.

It is important as a parent not to let our own feelings of fear or stress get to you. It is crucial to breathe and keep calm and not let them enmesh you in their circus that you end up shouting and screaming too. If that happens then you become like two two-year-olds having a fight. If you keep calm, you are better able to deal with the problem facing you. Focus on the issue, and don't go off at a tangent. What you want is for your teenager to come out of it with their self-esteem intact and that you have been able to parent your teen in a calm and kind manner, so that your teen can come to you if they are in trouble again. Each time it happens teach them to learn from it to help them self-regulate. The more they learn to self-regulate the less tantrums they will have. It will teach them to cope with their emotions better and ask for what they want instead of screaming it.

There is always a reason for the teenager without mental health issues, to act up. They may be in the wrong but they do not know it and do not feel it in the moment but may sincerely believe their point of view. They may be wrong but become defensive. Your job is to keep calm and help them calm down so that you get to a place where you can have a discussion without any shouting going on.

There may be other reasons for teens to act up; sometimes they can act withdrawn, and at other times, they can lash out or scream and shout. Ask them if you can, in the most tactful way if anyone is doing anything to them that they aren't happy with. You need to be aware that sexual abuse does exist and that even though you have done everything you can to keep your teen safe, that there are other adults in authority over them that can be abusing their position of trust. It is sad to have to say that, but it happens! Remind them that if anything untoward happens to them that they can always come to you and you will listen and help them. Remind them also that their body is their own and that no one can make them do what they do not want to do with their body. When they say NO, it's NO even if they have to fight the person to get away. Even if that is not the case, use the opportunity to have a conversation about it. Make them feel safe and that they can always come to you.

Teenagers can be very challenging to parents as they do not think like an adult does in different circumstances. They are neither child, nor are they an adult either; most teens are horrified if you treat them as a child, as many want to be treated more like an adult. However, they do not have the maturity of the adult. It can be a difficult time emotionally.

The problem comes when they do not have the adulthood to cope with their feelings; fear and anger can easily get the better of them. A lot depends on their level of maturity or whether they are using any substance of abuse which can cloud how they think. Smoking Marijuana, although most people feel that it will chill them, can trigger major anger in them at other times. It is the best demotivator I know! Another thing that teenagers do not think of is that smoking dope or taking any substance of abuse can trigger mental illness, even though they haven't done it much. It's best not to go there, especially if there are genetic risk factors for mental illness in the family.

At the teenage stage of their development, the rational part of their brain tends to give way to the more emotional and reactive part of their brain, which is why it is easy for teens to get easily fired up; and let's not forget the cocktail of hormones flooding their bodies as they are growing up, which can make them aggressive rather than assertive.

It is not until they reach the age of 25, that the human brain fully develops. When we understand this fact, we can also understand how teenagers can easily get into trouble.

We all know how an imbalance in our hormones can mess us around! During these growing up years, the teenage body is flooded with a huge influx of sex hormones and growth hormones, which can create a recipe for unstable mood swings and irrational behaviours.

Many teenagers can go through these awkward years well, as there are always exceptions to the rule, but many others may need more understanding and help to sort out their complex feelings.

Some helpful tips:

- When you talk to your teens you may need to be careful how you approach them. If you say anything critical, you will put their backs up straight away and there will be no point to have any discussion, because their aim will be to prove how unfair you truly are!
- It is best to describe the behaviour rather than call them a "not-so-nice-name", such as "liar" ... . yes, even if it's true! For instance, you can say: "You just said that you were at your friend's house, now you're saying that you went to a club. What did you really do?" Tell them that if they do not tell you

the truth, you will not know when you should believe them and when you shouldn't.

- Ask questions to get information and ask questions to try and get them to problem-solve, rather than accuse them. if you can't stand their mess. Tell them that you're finding it difficult to see all their clothes all over the floor and it makes it hard for you. How can they help with this problem? 'What can you do to help me?'
- Mind your language, definitely no cursing! keep calm, be non-judgemental, keep sarcasm away from your conversation and describe what you mean instead.
- If they are disrespectful, you can't demand that they give you respect, but you can ask them to behave in a respectful manner towards you.
- Define what you see as the problem in simple terms, so that you both understand each other. Be clear and concise. A lot of problems are easily solved when you define how they see the issue and then define how you see the matter. Then you can ask them how they think that you can come to a solution and listen to their suggestions. You don't have to agree with them if it's not the right solution, but make sure that they see that you have heard them and considered their suggestion. You can choose to offer a compromise or ask them to do what you think the right solution is to the problem.
- If you want to solve the problem, do not compare them to their friend, who is so good and do not criticize them.
- You can make a list of what you see as the behaviour problem. Be truthful and keep it non-judgemental. (If you can't prove something don't challenge them about it until you have proof). If you do, they will use this to show you that what you are saying is just not true and feel justified in their argument. This will help deviate the conversation from the point you want to make. Do not forget that you are talking to

a very intelligent teen, who by now has learnt to manipulate perhaps! Keep to the point!

- You can keep a record of how often and how bad the behaviours have occurred over the last fortnight. That way when the behaviour improves you can also point that out or if it gets worse you can plan what you're going to do about it. In a way, it's a means of tracking their behaviour and your teen may think twice about doing it again if they know that it's written down and they would have to be responsible for the consequences of their behaviour.

- Discuss and describe in details what you expect them to do. For instance, no fighting, swearing or screaming; to come straight back home after school. So, if school finishes by 3.30pm and it takes 10 minutes to get home, you will be expecting them by 3.40-3.45pm.

- Make sure that you keep your cool, be precise, keep your voice neutral and speak clearly but with confidence. That way, you can paraphrase and make sure that you have both understood each other exactly and what is expected of them.

- Reward good behaviour. Explain the rules, expectations and reward to your teen. Make sure that they have fully understood you. Discuss the reward with them. Make the reward something that they value and something they cannot get by themselves, but it must be really important to them, otherwise there is no incentive for them to improve.

- You can write out a "little contract" between you. If your teen keeps their part of the bargain, you also promise the reward that you have both chosen. Make sure that what you are asking of them is achievable by them and it is not too hard to accomplish especially at the beginning, so that they feel that it's worth it; otherwise, if it's too hard, they can feel hopeless and easily give up as they feel that can never achieve it anyway, so why bother?

- Put your little contract somewhere where it can be easily seen every day by your teen. It may be good to remind them of the expected reward if they are thinking of going off the rail. The thought of getting their reward may be enough to keep them on the straight and narrow! Rewards can include money... perhaps to accumulate to buy something that's important to them, Wi-Fi access, access to the phone, later bedtime, meeting a friend etc. You need to be in control of the reward and the teen need to strive to earn the reward.

- Don't start the new rule until the next day, as it is better to have a fresh start.

- Whatever you both decided on, you need to keep your word and follow through with it no matter what, otherwise you will lose credibility with your teen.

- You need to keep ahead of the behaviour so that you can check whether your plan is working or not. If you relax your teen will not believe you any longer; you will be giving them your power and they will feel in control of you instead.

- You may find that you made a few mistakes in the first contract. So, you need to reassess as you go along to rectify any loopholes. If there is a loophole, they will find it! Your rules are not meant to be broken!

- As we are talking about teenagers, you need to be acutely aware of any physical, emotional or psychological changes that as parents you may notice but then let it go and think that it's your imagination. If your subconscious picks up something, question it. Don't live in denial.

- If they are losing weight, there is a reason for it.

- If they're putting on weight, there is a reason for that too.

- If their pupils are dilated or pinpoint, there is a reason for that. Ask the right questions. It may be that they have started to smoke Cannabis or take some other drug or using alcohol. Don't ignore it. Check it out. Never be embarrassed to ask.

- If you're not sure take them to your doctor as a first port of call and ask the questions.
- If they are having mood swings, there is a reason for that too. Don't ignore it.
- Check if they are feeling down, irritable or withdrawn or if there are signs of depression or that they may be being bullied.
- Bullying can present itself in the physical, mental, psychological, emotional or cyber bullying.
- If they are on social media, you need to be their "friend" so that you know if there is anything that may be worrying your teenager, and know who they are talking to, and that it's safe for them. You need to monitor their activity on social media.
- Keep an eye on their circle of friends, and make sure that they are a good influence on your teen.
- Before they go on social media you need to have a conversation with them and warn them about the dangers of cyber bullying or predators and how dangerous that can be. Make sure they know to let you know straight away if anything derogatory or untoward is written against them. You want to prevent cyber bullying at all costs. Teach them about the delete button and blocking someone. You also need to check if there are any predators that are targeting your teen on the internet and making themselves pass as another teenager; check if they are secretly talking with someone. Nothing should be done in secret.
- Encourage your teenager and take care that they have good self-esteem. They will cope better with anyone who is trying to bully them physically or on the internet, if their self-esteem is in good shape.
- Make sure that both parents are on the same page. Show your teenager that you have a united front and that you are

working together for their benefit and that you are always open to have any conversation with them.

- But most of all, cultivate your relationship with your teen so that they feel that they can come to you with whatever is concerning them.

Parents need to fill a child's bucket of self-esteem so high that the rest of the world can't poke enough holes to drain it dry.

- Lessons Learnt in Life/fb page

CHAPTER THIRTEEN

Some Parenting Challenges

Part 5

Bullying

Bullying and harassment are difficult and dreaded topics for any parent and has become an increasing issue more and more in schools across the country. The problem is that bullying can start in kindergarten. The idea that our little ones can be bullied strikes fear in many parents' hearts and they don't know what to do and how to react. To have to deal with bullying in the pre-schoolers can be very confronting for parents.

The problem is that domestic violence these days is increasing and is a hot topic at present. The thing is that children live what they see and what they experience. If they are the victims of violence at home or seen one parent being ill-treated by the other, they may re-enact what they have seen on other children. It may not even be domestic violence as such but if the child has parents who react crudely to each other, the child can copy that same crude behaviour at kindergarten on a poor unsuspecting child.

It is common for younger children to repeat language that they've heard, without fully understanding what they are talking about and the implications of what they meant. Nevertheless, your child is then in contact with a behaviour or language that you may not approve of.

The children who are harassed or hassled or worried may be so distraught that they may develop a strong fear or anxiety. Other children can also feel intimidated and not know how to respond or behave if they see another child being bullied. They may be very scared of reprisals against themselves, and therefore turn the other way or turn a blind eye.

If you suspect anything, you must contact the school and work with them to stop the bullying. Do not approach the child or parent. It is best to let the ones in authority to deal with them. The bullying child himself needs help as he may be bullied at home himself.

If you have taught your children how to be positive, optimistic and confident, they are less likely to be bullied than the shy ones.

Bullies always look for a weak spot to have a go at someone. They will look for something that's different so that they can have a go at them. If the child is shy and easily embarrassed, and lacks confidence, they will pick on him; if the child is carrying a bit more weight than his peers, they may not be so confident and the bullies will discover that weak spot where they can get leverage from. If your child is an anxious one, the bullies will see this as weakness and target them. If the child reacts with fear to any of their taunts, they will use them as one of their victims and will keep at it.

So, you need to arm your children and equip them well for school life. It is law that your child needs to be educated and attend school. If you start to give in to the child and let them miss school days, you are on a long road to many more difficulties. In fact this will encourage their anxiety.

Teach your child how to listen well and respect other people's point of view. Teach them how "not" to take the "bait" and how not to overact and not show fear. That's what the bullies are looking for. They are looking for someone to react to their aggravating tactics. Learning to react "low key" no matter how aggravated they feel will stand them in good stead.

If your child is interested in martial arts, it may be a good thing to enrol them let's say in Karate or Tai Kwando, but stress that it is not to be used on anyone, but the training will make them stronger and build their confidence. However, if they know they have some skills in blocking others from hurting them, it may be give them more self-assurance in themselves and bullies are less likely to pick on them.

Children have a natural curiosity about other children, who fall into a different category other than their own. Bullies tend to target other children who are different from the crowd. As previously discussed, if children learn to accept and respect others from a young age, they are more likely to be more accepting of different customs and ways. Teach them about different cultures, religions and traditions and the importance of respecting each other to live in peace together. Many children are easily drawn to helping other children especially; for instance, recently, many young children from a local school cut their long hair to help make wigs for cancer patients as one of their friends suffered with cancer. You can but applaud these brave and generous children as many of them would have been very attached to their beautiful long locks! It would have done much to raise those children self-esteem however.

Younger children tend to see things as either good versus bad; older children develop more sophisticated distinction in thinking, moral and intellectual reasoning.

The Net

As much as the internet can create such addiction to it that it steals quality time with your children and your family, it is also an extremely useful tool for young people, people in the work force, or even the older generation to go to, to search for information or get connected. It is now impossible to have a business without the use of the internet. Unfortunately, many good things have a not so good side to them. Nowadays, the internet can be used as a weapon by bullies or sex predators.

This phenomenon has just gotten worse and worse over the last 20 years. Sex predators have become very sophisticated in using the internet to reach young teenagers, often by pretending to be a young teenager themselves.

Parents today need to learn new skills to cope with all these dangers and challengers facing their young people. There are no real rules or guidelines on how to surf the net safely. It is an open door where anything goes. Children and teenagers come across information that they are not prepared for or have no idea how to deal with it, which is why parents need to be vigilant with their children and their time on the net monitored.

We are in an era where instant messaging, chat rooms, emails, and social media are the norms. We no longer pick up the phone to have a chat with someone. We message them and expect an immediate answer back. Unfortunately, these sites form a great platform for bullies and sex predators.

It could also be that it was previously as bad, but many didn't report it or were too scared of the repercussions of reporting it, as every day almost, we are hearing about sexual crimes being revealed that happened twenty years ago. However, we have become acutely aware that sex predators have become more and more sophisticated in using the internet to target young children and teenagers.

As parents you need to educate yourself with new skills and acquire resources to cope with all these dangers and challenges facing children. You have to be aware of all the dangers that a young person can encounter on the net.

Sadly, these internet sites are a great platform for bullies and sex predators to reach young people. As a parent it is vital for you to know what your young people are up to on the net and who they are talking to. There are sites where you have the parental control and that your teenager cannot reach without your permission. It is good to keep an eye on who they are talking to and what they are reading and watching on their computer. On the other hand, teenagers too are very knowledgeable about computers and have discovered ways of overriding their parental control, which is one of the main reasons why computers should be in a place where the parents can keep an eye on what they are up to.

On the other hand, it is imperative for a young person to be able to access the internet for their education as well as keeping in touch with their friends. But these should not in any way be secretive.

The sad fact is that many teenagers have taken their own lives due to cyber bullying. This is another reason for parents to be vigilant and know what's going on online with their teenagers.

In today's society, it is imperative for young people to be "computer-savvy" no matter what field they choose to study or work in. It is expected of them to have computer skills as we live in this technological age.

Technology is an essential skill to acquire however, spending time on the internet can be fraught with danger for young people due to cyber bullying and sex predators, who may even plan to abduct their victims. It is a real dilemma for parents to keep their children and young people safe at the same time as encouraging them to learn and prosper. This is not to panic you but to raise awareness that the innocent computer that we all so need can be a weapon to be used against your children.

To some parents, their children's expertise in technology can be very intimidating, especially if they don't understand their jargon and can't keep up with the speed with which their children can perform their tasks. So, how do parents find balance?

We all know how easy it is to spend hours on social media when we were just checking something. As I've said before, technology is as addictive as drugs.

"One is addicted to something when we have a compulsive, biological, physical and psychological need to have more of something".

"Addiction is characterized by inability to consistently abstain, impairment in behavioural control, craving, diminished recognition of significant problems with one's behaviours and interpersonal relationships, and a dysfunctional emotional response. Like other chronic diseases addiction often involves cycles of relapse and remission. Without treatment or engagement in recovery activities, addiction is progressive and can result in disability or premature death" (Quoted from Public Policy Statement: Definition of Addiction).

"In Addiction the brain reward centre, the Dopamine centre, is constantly being triggered by an activity; very soon, the need for the reward becomes stronger and stronger, so that if you are addicted to cigarettes, you need to smoke more; if you are addicted to drugs or alcohol, you need to keep increasing your intake to achieve the same pleasurable effect. If you're addicted to gambling, you need to keep gambling more and more as your brain is expecting to be rewarded. Even if you've just lost a huge amount of money, your brain will tell you to play one more time as it could be the time that you will win! In reality, you end up losing more and more but still your pleasure centre is calling you to have another go! That's addiction!"

If you're addicted to technology, you need more and more time in front of your I.T screens, to achieve the pleasurable effect which is driving you.

The Raise Institute notes that online addiction is the inability to control the amount of time interfacing with digital technology and the need for more time or a new game to achieve a desired mood.

As parents you have to keep a close eye on your teens and check how much time they are spending online.

- Be aware that online addiction can cause them to withdraw from family and friends and their social life.
- Watch their academic performance and make sure that they are not dropping their grades.
- Keep a close eye over their overall health and wellbeing; that they are not constantly tired, dark circles around the eyes, or looking pale as they have no outdoor activities.

- Keep an eye on their diet.
- Ensure that they have adequate sleep. If you can't trust them with the computer or other technology in their bedrooms, they will all have to come out of the bedroom. Preferably the computer needs to be in an open place where the parents can keep an eye on what's going on.

So, how do you know that your teens are addicted to being online, especially if you have no one to compare with?

First of all, after a while you will start by being disturbed that your teenager is spending more and more time online or in their bedroom, and not wanting to participate in family activities, but instead they are on their phones, tablet, computer etc. As it is a common problem that teenagers often retreat to their bedrooms, you may not be sure if it's really a problem or just you worrying unnecessarily, which is another reason that the computer needs to be out of the bedroom. You need to have a frank conversation with your teen and continue to be vigilant about their behaviour, limit their time on the net when they are not studying and watching for cyber-bullying.

As technology has marched on so quickly and keep developing at the rate of knots, this is a new era for parents to cope with. One, that other generations haven't had to face until now. Like it or not, technology is everywhere, into all aspects of our lives and we are very grateful for the convenience. If we do not keep up with it, we get left behind.

Tips when to be concerned:

- Your teens are spending more time talking to virtual friends and neglecting their real friends.
- If your teens are constantly breaking your online rules.
- If you notice tantrums or massive mood swings if they can't get online.

- If they are constantly tired, have dark circles under the eyes; maybe staying up till late on the computer.
- If they are getting more and more withdrawn and can't be bothered with people.
- If their grades at school/university are dropping.

As technology is very much part and parcel of the world we live in, it is important from the start to have ground rules about technology. Your need to fully understand and stick to your boundaries. However, if you have a teen that's spending more and more time online, you need to tackle them straight away and find out why. It could be genuine that they have to do some research for their education. Make sure that you don't come across as too authoritarian, judgemental or as patronising. They will tell you that you are old school and that you don't understand!

- If you lay down the rules they could rebel and make your life and the life of everyone else's a misery. Being too harsh can lead to resentment and unhappiness.
- When you decide on house rules, it applies to everyone in the household including you. Be careful not to break your own house rules as they will no longer respect what you say.
- Decide the house rules that technology is not used during lunch and dinner time, or on waking prior to going to school/college/Uni.
- It is best to discuss this with your teens and get them to agree and commit to it. If they do, you can later on get them to commit to bigger things.
- Be consistent with its implementation.
- If they break the rules, there has to be consequences to pay.
- Select a time in the week for family bonding time. Teach your children that family time is very important and that everyone needs to participate. Take time in the week to involve the whole family and get everyone involved and make it fun and

something to look forward to. Cancel other things which coincide with family time if at all possible. Encourage your children to be part of the decision-making in how they want to spend their family time. For example: Playing a board game, doing a sports activity together like kayaking, watching a film together, going out for a meal together, going for walks, to the cinema etc. Of course, during family time no devices are allowed.

- Use these opportunities for parents, teenagers and younger children to bond together further, which will allow you to have an insight in how your children or teens are thinking; learn what's important to them and what they really care about and what their ambitions are. Allow them the time to talk while you listen. If they have these close bonds with you and the family, they are less likely to allow others to bully them or they are more likely to alert you straight away.

- These regular family contacts with a purpose will help your teenagers and children to appreciate and value their family and understand that there is more to life than playing virtual games with virtual friends who don't really exist.

- If they have assignments due in, help them to make a plan when they will sit down and do them rather than leave them till the last minute and rush them. That way they will not be giving their best.

- Teach them by example and discussions about relationships and how to relate with their mother, father and siblings and about the importance of unity in the family and having happy relationships together.

- These exercises help them to manage their time better as they will know what to expect during the week and may look forward to the weekly family gatherings.

Initially, there may be reluctance on your children's part, but keep going with it as it will eventually become a family pattern that everyone looks forward to. From time to time, check on their goals and remind them what they wish to achieve and redirect their path if they are straying from it.

If you think that your teen is addicted to technology, use their addiction to turn it to good use. If they are very smart with technology encourage them to help someone else (maybe, one of your friends) design their website or may be to get them to further their knowledge by doing further training in programming or designing. This way they are using what they like to further fulfil their ambitions and to be productive.

As technology seem to all happen indoors, encourage your teenager to have regular exercise as it is laying down foundations for lasting life-long habits. If, for instance they have a regular long bike ride with a couple of friends and come back exhausted they will be less likely to stay up all night on their phone, game console or computer most of the night.

Encourage them to see friends who do not have the same techno-addicted problem. Teenage years are difficult years where adolescents often feel awkward and uncomfortable. If possible, encourage them to socialise with family friends' teenagers and do some activities together, which, of course, doesn't involve technology. Encourage them to see other college/university friends for a game of tennis, table tennis, squash, golf or some other social activity which they enjoy. These encounters will also help them to develop their social skills by conversing and interacting with adults and other teens and practice their social graces.

Research notes that satisfied parents are those who are engaged in all aspects of their children's lives; and also, that these parents did not rely on technology but a range of other techniques to guide and supervise their children's online behaviour.

If children are low in self-esteem, they are more likely to feel affected by what people say about them, than children who have good self-esteem and are confident. Timid children are a greater target for bullies and these can almost rely on the shy ones not to blow their cover as bullies, because they would be too terrified in case of reprisals.

Cyber bullying comprises mainly of verbal hostility and aggression such as threatening or distressing electronic communications. These bullies often indirectly attack their victims mainly through social media platforms to spread rumours and destroy the reputation of their target person.

The young people bullied feel even worse as they know that all their friends and all their contacts on social media have also read dreadful things about them and that they may believe that the lies are true. These bullies may go as far as destroying their victim's property. They can be ruthless. These behaviours are criminal and can have repercussions in the criminal justice.

I cannot stress enough how very damaging bullying is to a child. As a Life Coach I see many adults whose problems started by being bullied at school. This degrading experience marks them for many, many years and sometimes for life. Not only does the experience of being bullied can be extremely distressing to a child or young person, but the damage continues to occur to them for years and years after the actual bullying has ceased. It is not surprising that we have lost many teenagers to suicide due to cyber bullying.

The current definition acknowledges two modes and four types by which youth can be bullied or can bully others.

The two modes of bullying include "Direct" (e.g. bullying that occurs in the presence of a targeted youth) and "Indirect" (e.g. bullying not directly communicated to targeted youth such as spreading rumours).

In addition to these two modes, the 4 types of bullying include broad categories of physical, verbal, relational (e.g. efforts to harm the reputation or relationships of the targeted youth), and damage to property. (Taken from the net).

Most of us are aware about some types of bullying, however, today, bullying has become very sophisticated, due to our progress in technology. It can be through the phone, without even having to talk to their target, due to text messages, or through emails, chat rooms, and online posts through social media. Sometimes these can be relentless, enough to drive a youth with low self-esteem to suicide, as it has been proven on many occasions.

As stated, cyber bullying can involve verbal aggression, such as threatening or harassing electronic communications and relational aggression such as spreading rumours electronically.

As noted in the definition of cyber bullying, it can even go further than that "by involving property damage resulting from electronic attacks that lead to modification, dissemination or destruction of their target's privately stored information".

Many of these can be classified as criminal activities such as harassment and assault. I believe that any kind of bullying as such is criminal! Bullying doesn't only involve a one-time incident, it usually involves repeated incidents. Unfortunately, the internet has made it easy for those cowards to harass and stalk their victims, many without any repercussions.

A child or young person who is being bullied tends to live in fear of the bully or bullies and it is extremely difficult for them to feel safe again or relax once the bullies have got to them. They are anxious, even when the bully is not within their proximity. Some become paranoid or suffer with anxiety attacks and depression. This is why as parents, you need to be very alert and notice any changes in your young people. Don't let life's other stressors blind you to what's happening with your child.

On the other hand, bullying isn't only reserved for children. It can happen to people of all ages and different backgrounds and in different situations, for example in the work place.

Research in 2013 by Safe Work Australia found out that Australia has the highest workplace bullying rates all over the world. The report also stated that Australian employers lost $8 billion a year due to absenteeism and sickness, of which 693 million were caused by workplace bullying.

One needs to ask: What has been done since to rectify this situation?

Younger Children

Many younger children also get targeted by bullies at school. They may not be of an age where they can be cyber bullied, but the damage can be as deep and profound.

All report of bullying or harassment must be taken seriously by the parents and by the school.

All schools have bullying policies and protocols in place.

It is extremely distressing, upsetting and stirs up anger inside of all of us when you think that some awful child is bullying your little angel. Your natural instinct is to march down to the school and demand an explanation and a promise that it will never happen again! However, it is very important for your child that as their parents that you stay calm and remain positive. Your child may be panicked and stop you from speaking to the teacher or to the Principal. Nevertheless, it's important that you do so; reassure your child as much as possible but if they still don't want you to talk with the school, you don't need their permission to do it but give them the confidence to know that you are now aware, you are on their side and that you will work to get it sorted out and that they need not be concerned. This is not to say that they will take your word for it. You will have to do a lot of reassuring.

The decision is not your child's; it is your decision to make.

- If your child's safety is threatened, you must make it a priority. It's important to talk with the school. Sometimes a self-confident, positive and resilient appearance of both parents (unless you are a single parent; however, you can take a friend with you) at the school is enough to stop the bullying from continuing.

- Being aggressive only complicates matters and makes the school believe that you will not cooperate with them. Be assertive, not aggressive.
- Keep your focus on finding a solution to the problem. Don't allow yourself to get emotionally hijacked and overreact to everything, and let it cloud your judgement. Keep your feelings of anger, hurt, and upset till you get home .... but not in front of your child. Keep your calm.
- Aim to be part of the solution, not the problem.
- If you have other parents as friends at school, make sure that you build yourself a little support network for yourself and for their child to gently be kept an eye on by playing with their real friends.
- It is not your job to punish the bully or to tackle the child's or children's' parents; it's best left to the school to cope with. They are not emotionally involved.
- Do everything you can to help the school to come to a reasonable solution. The best outcomes are achieved when your child feels comfortable that home and school work together.

CHAPTER FOURTEEN

Some Parenting Challenges

Part 6

To smack or not to smack

Smack your child every day. If you don't know why – he does.

- Joey Adams

Nowadays, this is an age-old debate, to which everyone has a strong opinion about! Some are absolutely anti-smacking and others have no problem with it. Those who smack their children feel very judged by those who do not and vice versa.

The thing is if we are asking this question of an older group of people, they would be saying to you, that they were smacked and very proudly tell you that they came out alright and that a smack never did them any harm. This can be true enough, because in those days, it was the only deterrent that parents had to keep their children in line and discipline them. Why?...... because we didn't know any other ways of correcting children or of getting them to do what the parents wanted. However, it doesn't mean that it is the only way or that it is even the right thing to do.

How children are smacked, makes the difference. If the parent gives a small smack on the bottom or the back of the hand, not in anger, but to chastise the child when they do wrong, so that the child understands that they must not repeat that action again, seem to be more acceptable to society than if the smack is given in anger and with force. A smack that leaves marks on the child's skin, one given with an angry tone and makes the child feel belittled, that scenario is not so easily tolerable by society today. The child then lives in fear of being smacked again. This scenario is possibly no more than what a bully would do. I'm bigger and stronger than you, so I can hit you, if you don't do what I asked you to do!

On the other hand, many anti-smackers have not had other skills put in place, to discipline their children. Consequently, many children who have never had a smack from their parents may have grown up undisciplined with no fear of any consequences whatsoever, which then leads many to question whether a controlled smack given at the right time, without anger, can be the right way to go? The problem also is that it doesn't teach the children about consequences of their actions and their responsibilities towards them.

There is equally the point that if the children do not respect their parents because they do not fear any consequences, then they may treat other adults or authority figures in that same vein. The consequence of this, means that those children show no respect for teachers, their boss, the law or any other authority figures that they happen to come across and that others have to abide to in our culture.

So, what we are saying here is that a small smack, to gently remind a child that they need to toe the line is not exactly "corporal punishment". Words are very powerful, when we call a small controlled smack "corporal punishment" or "violence towards a child", we are then hyping people's emotions and we all react on an emotional level rather than reacting to the "so-called crime" we are discussing, for example, a gentle smack to teach your child perhaps not to run across the road again and get themselves killed. None of us would want to see a child harmed. In fact, if we are to see a child who is being harmed, it is our duty to do something about it and report it.

The problem with smacking years ago, was that many children were corrected by a form of "real" corporal punishment. It may mean that the child was beaten with a leather belt or a wooden object. They were even allowed to be smacked with a ruler or maybe something else at school, as a form of punishment. Those generations of children did suffer under the guise of discipline. Just because we did things that way in the 1950s let's say, doesn't exactly mean that we should be doing the same thing in the years 2018. We have moved from the era where corporal punishment was not only acceptable but essential, to a time where smacking is very frowned upon to offering nothing in its place or maybe very little.

However, in today's society, more skills are being offered to young parents or carers to help discipline their children, for instance, the proper use of Time-Out. On the other hand, even the pro-smackers feel guilty and regret smacking their children when they had to. Then there is the question whether it is effective to smack our children. If our children do not perform a certain behaviour out of fear of being smacked, it is not the smacking that is effective it the fear of being smacked again because it hurts physically and it hurts the child's pride, which does nothing for the child's self-esteem. Smacking can build resentment. Smacking your child will not cause permanent damage to your child if you balance it with your usual care and love and praise towards your child when they behave well. On the other hand, smacking may damage your relationship with your child if you solely rely on smacking to discipline your child. Some can feel abused and plan to get their own back on their parents as they get older.

Some tips:

- Threats and smacking do not work especially if the parent is not consistent.
- It can be useful to count **One, Two, Three**: In other words, one is a soft warning. Two is a firmer warning and at Three you can show that you are angry and mean business and

carry out the punishment. This tends to work very well with toddlers.

- Often when your child is whining or acting up, they are just attention-seeking. So, even when you smack your child for acting up or whining, you will not stop the bad behaviour because when you smack them, you are giving them your full attention, which is what they wanted in the first place; but they have learnt to get this attention in a very negative way. Negative attention is still attention! It is far better than to be ignored for the child!

- It is important for you to address the bad behaviour and reward the good behaviour. Let's say, when your child is whining and you want them to stop, you can say: "Use your words properly, then Mummy can understand you"; and when they do, reward them with hugs and praise to encourage them to speak properly the next time. If the next time, the whining starts again, you can remind them how wonderful they were when they used their words properly to make Mummy understand what they wanted and how much Mummy was pleased with them. Before you know it, they will stop whining because you gave the good behaviour the emphasis and the reward needed, instead of concentrating on the behaviour you didn't want to see.

- If you use smacking on an on-going basis daily, it can be quite detrimental to your relationship with your child, and it won't work. Resentment builds up and it has been known for some to think of getting their revenge once they're older.

- If you smack in anger or frustration, you have already lost that battle! You lost control. This happens because you don't know what else to do.

- If you are to admonish your child, get down to their level so that you can give them good eye contact and that they know exactly what has displeased you so much and can see what you are saying to them. Otherwise you may be towering over them and appear like a giant to them, which can be very intimidating. What you are saying becomes secondary and they do not take it in.

- Speak softly, let them know that their action was intolerable, and tell them what you're going to do about it.
- Remember that if you have a school-aged child, they are being given instructions from the time they get up to the time they go to bed and that can be confusing for them. So, when you give instructions to your children be clear and make sure that the child has understood you before you get angry with them. Depending on their age, make sure that you don't ask them to do too many things at once and that they can't remember what they are supposed to do next. They can't tell you that's what's happening because they are the child and you are the parent; the adult who is supposed to understand them. Don't ask a two-year old, to go upstairs, put his pyjamas on, bring his book down and clear up his toys. After going upstairs and perhaps remembering to put on his pyjamas, he would have forgotten the rest of your instructions.
- Rather than lashing out with a smack, using One, Two, Three or Time-out are good skills to put in place so that the child knows what is acceptable and what is not. Using praise to modify behaviour is also very useful.

The upshot of it, is, that smacking is outdated and it doesn't work. It can cause resentment and incite children to take their revenge when they are older. Research tells us that children who ended up as well-adjusted adults were treated consistently, predictably and fairly in childhood.

CHAPTER FIFTEEN

Children's self-esteem

Low self-esteem is often created by what others call us or say about us and we end up believing them.

When we don't feel good about who we are, we are not happy. No matter how well things are going in other areas of our lives, we can't be happy if we don't like ourselves or feel good about who we are. It is the same way with children. We are in control of our children's self-esteem up to a point when they are still very small, as they are mainly in our full-time care before others such as kindergarten, school, friends, or some other formal influence can't get to them. It is important for you to be aware of keeping your children's self-esteem intact whilst you, as parents, are the only influence in their lives.

Never believe that your pre-school child would do something that displeases you out of malice, although it may seem so at times. Children do not have the maturity to think in such a negative way. It's only an adult brain who has lived life for many years and has learnt sometimes negative behaviours along the way that can think that way. Their brains and emotions are still very young and fresh and innocent and are not capable of thinking in an adult manner as they have not had the experience to learn from it.

Babies do not see themselves as separate from their mothers when they are first born. They just see themselves as an extension of their mothers. However, the way you care for your baby prepares the ground work for their own self-esteem later on, by being gentle, speaking to them in a soothing way, attending to their cries, pampering them with lots of love and cuddles and attending to their needs.

This prepares your baby to know that they are loved and cared for. Giving their grandparents or other family members the chance to be able to have regular access to them and show their love, also teaches them that not only do my parents love and care for me but there are other family members who love and care for me too, therefore giving them strong feelings of love and security.

The more people who love your child, the better it is for their self-esteem and their feelings of security.

So, be generous with your babies towards your parents and other family members. Your babies are the ones who will benefit from all that love and care and attention. Don't worry that your baby will love someone else more than you. It will never happen! Babies know instinctively who their mum and dad are and even their grandparents, and they will love no one else the way they love you! Ever! So, it's safe, be kind and generous towards your family members.

Remember, it takes a village to bring up a child! It is a little natural to feel a bit possessive to start with but the more you entertain that way of thinking, the worse it will get and I hate to say it, a bit selfish! The only loser will be you and your baby. Your family will be so bawled over by your generosity that you will benefit greatly yourself. If you keep yourself to yourself and do not allow other family members in, your baby and yourself will miss out on very precious love and care from others and it will do nothing to improve your self-esteem and that of your child.

Self-esteem is what we think of ourselves and liking ourselves. For children it means appreciating that they are loved and cared for by their nuclear family, and that they belong and are valued as a member of their families.

As their parents and carers', your children come with a clean slate. You can write great things on their slate, by being positive, by treating them well and praising them and treating them with respect, praise and attention and your children will have great self-esteem and behave appropriately. If they know that they are loved by their extended family, it will also raise their self-esteem. They will be happy children and feel that all is well with the world.

You could write a "mission statement" when they are still babies about how you will treat them in their childhood and keep it in mind as they grow up.

On the other hand, if you are possessive of them but treat them in a critical or negative way and do not take care that your children are absorbing your negative patterns that is going on around them, they may develop fears and anxiety and low self-esteem.

Toddlers start appreciating who they are, when they can understand what they can do and what makes them that individual little toddler. Often at 2 or 3 years old, a toddler will try and assert their independence by telling you that "I can do it all by myself!" or "I'm a big girl now". It is good to give them safe options like what they want to wear or give them a choice of two things that they want to eat. The decisions that they come to, is all part of the building blocks of their self-esteem. However, at that age, children do not see themselves through their own eyes, but they see themselves through your eyes, which is why parents have a huge role to play in building their children's self-esteem.

If you want to lead a quality life, there is one vital ingredient that is essential to your success. That ingredient is self-esteem, which is crucial to your happiness and success in life; that's why it is vitally important to preserve your children's self-esteem.

Our self-esteem can take years to build up and can be squashed in the blink of an eye. That's why it's important whilst our children are still small to pay attention to their self-esteem. That doesn't mean that we can let them get away with murder! But they have to be told right from wrong from the very start in a kind and understanding manner, which doesn't chip away at their self-esteem.

No child is born with low self-esteem

It is what happens to them during their childhood that makes them have good or poor self-esteem. You may find that your child's self-esteem changes as they get older. They may need different types of support at different developmental age groups to continue to build their self-esteem, depending on their personality.

Although we all know what we look like and what our children look like, your young babies and toddlers are only just discovering what they look like. This is why some mothers often say that their babies are very vain and love to look at themselves in the mirror. For them, everything is new. They are looking at everything with new eyes. So, they will love to see themselves in the mirror, otherwise they can't make out what they look like. A mirror can be a very friendly toy to a baby or toddler who can spend hours looking at themselves. When they discover that they can do some things they are very proud of themselves and are building up that self-esteem.

They are also working out where they belong, often by turning to their loved ones for cuddles and comfort. Sometimes, they go through developmental phases where they don't like something or someone who is unfamiliar, like a man with glasses or a moustache, if their own father doesn't look like that. They rely on your reactions; if you are reassuring they will get used to it eventually, but if you react in horror they will not have a bar of these people and cry every time.

By the time they reach 3 years old, they have learned an awful lot and their language skills can amaze you "actually"! They now understand that their bodies and minds are their own. If they have had good beginnings, most children can cope with being away from home for a little while, because they feel safe and know that they are loved. They like to know at that age, that they are the best at whatever they do as they now know how to compare themselves with their peers.... and sometimes think that they are the boss!

Children who are clingy to their mums and forever seeking them are perhaps those who possibly do not see their mum enough for whatever reason, or maybe is emotionally-distracted, leaving the child feeling insecure that their mum may be leaving them and can suffer with separation-anxiety; or it can also be that the mother feels flattered by being in such demand by their child that she encourages the clingy behaviour.

- To raise their self-esteem, it is important to give them some leeway and allow them to explore their environment, but they will look to you for reassurance if anything unusual happens. Your reaction will let them know if it's friend or foe!
- To help them develop a sense of self-confidence, it is quite okay to allow them to make small decisions, which give them a sense of being in control and raises their confidence and give them a sense of self.
- Toddlers fight to assert themselves, they like to decide who is in their game and who isn't. It's okay to allow them to say "NO", and to allow them to feel the consequences of their decisions.
- It is difficult for children to share with others before the age of two as they go through an Egoistic stage before 2; so, it comes quite hard for them to share when they are going through that stage. It is only through socialisation that they get to learn how to share. Teach them to take part in games and to share and take turns. They may not like it, but they have to learn the rules of socialisation all the same! Encourage them and praise them.

Pre-schoolers and self-esteem

If all is well, your pre-schoolers are able at this stage to stay away from home for a while if they feel loved and safe. They are also able to learn to accept some other adult to be in charge of them and respond well to the authority figure.

They like to compare themselves to others. They like to know that they're the best at what they do. It is up to us parents to keep their self-esteem intact by pointing out something that they are really good at but also helping them to realize that someone else is also good at something else. That way they feel proud of who they are and will try to do better too but appreciate others.

Primary school-age children and self-esteem

Primary school children start to realize that others may be better than them as they compare themselves with their friends and other children in their class. This may be the first test of their self-esteem.

School in itself can be quite stimulating for many by having to follow new rules and discipline from an authority figure who isn't Mum or Dad and having to learn new things. They themselves may realize that someone else is better at drawing that they are, but you can point out that they are better at running, which then raises their self-esteem which was in danger of taking a dive!

Some tips to help your primary schoolers:

- Be extra patient and keep your cool, especially at the end of a school day when your child is feeling exhausted. Give them plenty of love and cuddles. Being at school all day is exhausting! It takes a bit of getting used to!

- You can encourage them and point out their capabilities and talents and praise the efforts that they put in to their school work.

- Use praise to improve behaviour and enthusiasm. Focus on their good points and always tell them how proud you are of them.

- Coach your child about navigating difficult social situations and teach them to learn from their experiences.

- Teach them not to feel offended easily by others. It will save them a lot of upsets. Teach them to show willing and smile and other children are more likely to play with them instead than when they get upset. Show them how it's done by putting yourself in another child's shoe and role play with them.

- Teach your child about playing fair and about winning and losing.
- Teach them about generosity and teach them to forgive easily. When you forgive the little things, it gets easier to forgive the bigger things.
- It is important for your child to see that you and the school are working together and that there is no conflict between you. Keep in contact with the class teacher so that you can know how your child is doing and if there is a problem so that it can be sorted out immediately.
- Having a good relationship with the school is essential. If you can and have the time, get involved with the school, whether you can join the PTA, help with reading in class etc. That way, you will be more aware if there is any sign that your child is being bullied or has any other issues that can affect their self-esteem.
- At primary school self-esteem may be related to many different things, including their academic ability to learn, the way they look, whether they look different from the rest of their classmates, how good they are at sports or how popular they are with their little friends or not.

So, what is self-esteem?
Self-esteem is the thoughts you have about yourself. What you think of yourself.

What you believe about yourself, make it that you have a high self-esteem if you are at peace with yourself and appreciate yourself for who you are; or a low self-esteem, if you believe that you are not good enough and feel bad about yourself.

Self-esteem means appreciating yourself for who you are, warts and all. It is accepting yourself just as you are. Put in another way, it is acknowledging your strengths and weaknesses and feeling safe in that knowledge.

People with a healthy self-esteem, can feel good about who

they are, appreciate their own self-worth and take pride in their achievements and their gifts and talents, no matter how good or not they truly are. They make no apology for who they are. They understand that they are far from perfect, and that is okay with them as they do not chastise themselves over their weaknesses. They feel comfortable in their own skin.

Many clients come to me very aware that they suffer with low self-esteem. Strangely enough when questioned about it, many of them who have some insight into their life story, often know or have a good idea why they have low self-esteem or self-worth. Often, they relate it to an abusive or controlling relationship, often a parent, teacher or partner or to their conditioning and lack of love as a child. One would have thought that if they are conscious about the reasons why they are a certain way that they would be half-way in solving their self-esteem issues; but that is not the case.

Knowing what's wrong, is one thing, but doing something about it is quite another thing. Just because you are mindful about your problems, doesn't mean that you will automatically know what to do about them.

Very frequently, these childhood patterns are deeply ingrained in them. The process was set up for them a very long time ago by others and it isn't so easy for them to change if they are not given the tools to help them raise their self-esteem.

If you begin to notice that your child is suffering from poor self-esteem, it is crucial for you to find out more about them and do what you can do to raise their self-esteem. If you can't help your child, get professional help early. Things can be easily sorted out rather than having to deal with it many years later, when life becomes more complicated.

Lessons From Life

A child that Lives with Ridicule learns to be Timid.
A child that lives with Criticism learns to Condemn.
A child that lives with Distrust learns to be Deceitful.
A child that lives with Antagonism learns to be Hostile.
A child that lives with Affection learns to Love.
A child that lives with Encouragement learns Confidence.
A child that lives with Truth learns Justice.
A child that lives with Praise learns to Appreciate.
A child that lives with Sharing learns to be Considerate.
A child that lives with Knowledge learns Wisdom.
A child that lives with Patience learns to be Tolerant.
A child that lives with Happiness will find Love and Beauty.

- Ronald Russell

Conclusion

In conclusion this book has addressed some of the important issues that parents are faced with. So, as you can see the joy of parenting doesn't only bring joy; it can bring a lot issues that parents can struggle with! "The joys of parenting" is a two-edged sword. It brings immeasurable love and fun but it also brings its challenges at different stages of the parenting years.

As a parent, the more effort that you put into parenting your children, the more you will reap the happiness that having a great relationship with your children brings.

Having young children can be a difficult time for a lot of parents, as it is very common for parents to feel the tiredness that looking after them bring whilst navigating your other life's commitments.

Each stage of your children's childhood brings its own challenges. Many parents are keen to show to others that they are coping even when the going gets tough. There can be a lot of competition between parents themselves, to appear the best parents. If you need help, ask! Don't be too proud to ask for help. If you visit your GP or Child and Adolescent Clinic, they can direct you to the right people to help you. It will be well worth it

Your children will only ever have one childhood and there's no going back! Most parents who have children want to do the best they can for them. But often life takes over and stops us from being the best parent that we can be.

This can be due to ignorance or to our own poor childhood experiences. If our childhood has been less than ideal and we haven't had good role models, then we may struggle to get things right and may not know how to make things better.

It's never too late for you to get what you didn't have in your childhood. You can educate yourself and through aiming to give your own children the best childhood you can, you can relive your childhood through your children. You can experience love and satisfaction by being the best parent you can be and enjoy your children by pouring your love and efforts into them and reaping the benefits that they bring.

Thankfully, we have moved on from being the authoritarian parents and when smacking was all we knew how to get our children to do what we want them to do.

I do hope that you heed the warning about today's technology and its addiction. It is vital for your children to have emotionally available parents.

When parents are addicted to technology, everything else becomes secondary to it, including the children. Your children cannot get the best of who you are, and you cannot teach them what they vitally need for a healthy, happy childhood.

If you fake it, your children will know it. They have been programmed to study everything about you since they were born or even before. Take your responsibilities seriously and give them life-long good habits, avoid dramas and help them to be as creative as they can be. Be their best cheerleader!

I have tried to warn you about being entitled and to do your best not to pass this attitude to your children.

Instead, instil in them respect, empathy, forgiveness, humility, faith, compassion, love, resilience, confidence, an attitude of gratitude and much more. Teach your children to always do the right thing by the way you conduct your life.

As discussed, a lot of adults' mental illness start in childhood. So as a parent, you are given the privilege to take care of your children's mental health during their childhood. You can start by making sure that you respect and build up their self-esteem. Give your children the best childhood that they can possibly have. Your children are little adults in training. Don't forget, you are not bringing up children, you are preparing them to be adults who one day, will be self-reliable and know how to live the best life that they can independently. That will be your reward!

Good luck, God bless and hope that you enjoy your children's journey to adulthood.

Acknowledgements

A big thankyou to Sarah Perkins responsible for taking the photos and to Nathalie, Adam, Lucy and Benjamin Watson for appearing on the book cover.

Printed in the United States
By Bookmasters